FUTURE SEX

FUTURE SEX

EMILY WITT

ff

FABER & FABER

First published in the UK in 2017
by Faber & Faber Ltd
Bloomsbury House
74–77 Great Russell Street
London WC1B 3DA

First published in the USA in 2016
by Farrar, Straus and Giroux
18 West 18th Street
New York 10011

Printed and bound in the UK by CPI Group (UK) Ltd, Croydon CR0 4YY

The right of Emily Witt to be identified as the author of this work has been asserted in accordance with Section 77 of the Copyright, Designs and Patents Act 1988

Author's note: These are true stories, though some names have been changed

A CIP record for this book is available from the British Library

ISBN 978–0–571–33198–7

1 3 5 7 9 10 8 6 4 2

For my parents,

Leonard and Diana Witt

EXPLORATIONS

CONTENTS

CONTENTS

FUTURE SEX

EXPECTATIONS

I was single, straight, and female. When I turned thirty, in 2011, I still envisioned my sexual experience eventually reaching a terminus, like a monorail gliding to a stop at Epcot Center. I would disembark, find myself face-to-face with another human being, and there we would remain in our permanent station in life: the future.

I had not chosen to be single but love is rare and it is frequently unreciprocated. Without love I saw no reason to form a permanent attachment to any particular place. Love determined how humans arrayed themselves in space. Because it affixed people into their long-term arrangements, those around me viewed it as an eschatological event, messianic in its totality. My friends expressed a religious belief that it would arrive for me one day, as if love were something the universe owed to each of us, which no human could escape.

I had known love, but having known love I knew how

powerless I was to instigate it or ensure its duration. Still, I nurtured my idea of the future, which I thought of as the default denouement of my sexuality, and a destiny rather than a choice. The vision remained suspended, jewel-like in my mind, impervious to the storms of my actual experience, a crystalline point of arrival. But I knew that it did not arrive for everyone, and as I got older I began to worry that it would not arrive for me.

A year or two might pass with a boyfriend, and then a year or two without. In between boyfriends I sometimes slept with friends. After a certain number of years many of my friends had slept with one another, too. Attractions would start and end in a flexible manner that occasionally imploded in displays of pain or temporary insanity, but which for the most part functioned peacefully. We were souls flitting through limbo, piling up against one another like dried leaves, awaiting the brass trumpets and wedding bells of the eschaton.

The language we used to describe these relationships did not serve the purpose of definition. Their salient characteristic was that you had them while remaining alone, but nobody was sure what to call that order of connection. "Hooking up" implied that our encounters had no ceremony or civility. "Lovers" was old-fashioned, and we were often just friends with the people we had sex with, if not "just friends." Usually we called what we did "dating," a word we used for everything from one-night stands to relationships of several years. People who dated were single, unless they were dating someone. "Single" had also lost specificity: it could mean unmarried, as it did on a tax form, but unmarried people were sometimes not single but rather "in a relationship," a designation of provisional commitment for which we had no one-word adjectives. *Boyfriend, girlfriend,* or *partner* implied commitment and intention and therefore only served in certain instances. One friend referred to a "non-ex" with whom he had carried on a "nonrelationship" for a year.

Our relationships had changed but the language had not. In speaking as if nothing had changed, the words we used made us feel out of sync. Many of us longed for an arrangement we could name, as if it offered something better, instead of simply something more familiar. Some of us tried out neologisms. Most of us avoided them. We were here by accident, not intention. Whatever we were doing, nobody I knew referred to it as a "lifestyle choice." Nobody described being single in New York and having sporadic sexual engagement with a range of acquaintances as a "sexual identity." I thought of my situation as an interim state, one that would end with the arrival of love.

The year I turned thirty a relationship ended. I was very sad but my sadness bored everyone, including me. Having been through such dejection before, I thought I might get out of it quickly. I went on Internet dates but found it difficult to generate sexual desire for strangers. Instead I would run into friends at a party, or in a subway station, men I had thought about before. That fall and winter I had sex with three people, and kissed one or two more. The numbers seemed measured and reasonable to me. All of them were people I had known for some time.

I felt happier in the presence of unmediated humans, but sometimes a nonboyfriend brought with him a dark echo, which lived in my phone. It was a longing with no hope of satisfaction, without a clear object. I stared at rippling ellipses on screens. I forensically analyzed social media photographs. I expressed levity with exclamation points, spelled-out laughs, and emoticons. I artificially delayed my responses. There was a great posturing of busyness, of not having noticed your text until just now. It annoyed me that my phone could hold me hostage to its clichés. My goals were serenity and good humor. I went to all the Christmas parties.

The fiction that I was pleased with my circumstances lasted from fall into the new year. It was in March, the trees skeletal but thawing, when a man called to suggest that I get tested for a sexually transmitted infection. We'd had sex about a month before, a few days before Valentine's Day. I had been at a bar near his house. I had called him and he met me there. We walked back through empty streets to his apartment. I hadn't spent the night or spoken to him since.

He had noticed something a little off and had gotten tested, he was saying. The lab results weren't back but the doctor suspected chlamydia. At the time we slept together he had been seeing another woman, who lived on the West Coast. He had gone to visit her for Valentine's Day, and now she was furious with him. She accused him of betrayal and he felt like a scumbag chastised for his moral transgression with a disease. He'd been reading Joan Didion's essay "On Self-Respect." I laughed—it was her worst essay—but he was serious. I said the only thing I could say, which was that he was not a bad person, that we were not bad people. That night had been finite and uncomplicated. It did not merit so much attention. After we hung up I lay on the couch and looked at the white walls of my apartment. I had to move soon.

I thought the phone call would be all but then I received a recriminatory e-mail from a friend of the other woman. "I am surprised by you," it said. "You knew he was going to see someone and didn't let that bother you." This was true. I had not been bothered. I had taken his "seeing someone" as reassurance of the limited nature of our meeting, not as a moral test. "I would advise that you examine what you did in some cold, adult daylight," wrote my correspondent, who further advised me to "stop pantomiming thrills" and "starkly consider the real, human consequences of real-life actions."

The next day, sitting in the packed waiting room of a public health clinic in Brooklyn, I watched a clinician lecture her captive, half-asleep audience on how to put on a condom. We waited for our numbers to be called. In this cold, adult daylight, I examined what I had done. A single person's need for human contact should not be underestimated. Surrounded on all sides by my imperfect fellow New Yorkers, I thought many were also probably here for having broken some rules about prudent behavior. At the very least, I figured, most people in the room knew how to use condoms.

The clinician responded with equanimity to the occasional jeers from the crowd. She respectfully said "no" when a young woman asked if a female condom could be used "in the butt." After her lecture, while we continued to wait, public health videos played on a loop on monitors mounted on the wall. They dated from the 1990s, and dramatized people with lives as disorderly as mine, made worse by the outdated blue jeans they wore. The brows of these imperfect people furrowed as they accepted diagnoses, admitted to affairs, and made confessional phone calls on giant cordless phones. Men picked each other up in stage-set bars with one or two extras in fake conversation over glass tumblers while generic music played in the background to signify a party-like atmosphere, like porn that never gets to the sex. They later reflected on events in reality-television-style confessional interviews. From our chairs, all facing forward in the same direction, awaiting our swabbing and blood drawing, we witnessed the narrative consequences. (One of the men at the gay bar had a girlfriend at home . . . and gonorrhea. We watched him tell his girlfriend that he had sex with men and that he had gonorrhea.) The videos did not propose long-term committed relationships as a necessary condition of adulthood, just honesty. They did not recriminate. The New York City government had a technocratic view of sexuality.

The federal government had different expectations. Following the phone call I had looked up chlamydia on Google, which led me to the website for the Centers for Disease Control and Prevention. The government suggested that the best way to avoid chlamydia was "to abstain from vaginal, anal, and oral sex or to be in a long-term mutually monogamous relationship with a partner who has been tested and is known to be uninfected." It was a fantasy that defied interpretation, two cliffs without a bridge. The suggestion of abstinence came with a more realistic reminder to use condoms. I usually used condoms, but this time I had not used a condom, so now I used antibiotics. When the lab results came back days after my visit to the Brooklyn clinic it turned out I did not have chlamydia. None of us had chlamydia.

Like the federal government, I wanted nothing more than "a long-term mutually monogamous relationship with a partner who has been tested and is known to be uninfected." I had wanted it for a very long time, and it had not arrived. Who knew if it would one day happen? For now I was a person in the world, a person who had sexual relationships that I could not describe in language and that failed my moral ideals. Apprehensiveness set in: that this was my future.

On a Monday in April 2012, I stood in line at JFK Airport to board a plane to San Francisco. Before me stood a silver-headed West Coast businessman. His skin had the exfoliated, burnished sheen of the extremely healthy; his glasses were of an advanced polymer; he had dark jeans. He wore the recycled ethylene-vinyl acetate shoes that are said never to smell. His fleece coat was of an extraordinary thickness and quality, with a lissome external layer that would not pill. He seemed like the sort of man who would pronounce himself a minimalist and say that everything he bought was selected for its extraordinary craftsmanship and beautiful design. But the silver fox's computer bag was a cheap thing with netting and buckles that said GOOGLE on it. The person in front of him in line wore a Google doodle T-shirt with Bert and Ernie where the Os would be. In front of him was a Google backpack.

Until I left San Francisco it never went away. It was embroidered on breast pockets, illustrated with themes of America's cities, emblazoned on stainless-steel water bottles, on fleece jackets, on baseball caps, but not on the private buses that transported workers to their campus in Mountain View, where they ate raw goji-berry discs from their snack room and walked about swathed, priestlike, in Google mantles, with Google wimples and Google mitres, seeking orientation on Google Maps, googling strangers and Google-chatting with friends, as I did with mine, dozens of times a day, which made the recurrence of the logo feel like a monopolist taunt.

My first day in the city I sat in a sunlit café in the Mission, drank a cappuccino, and read a paper copy of the *San Francisco Chronicle* that lay anachronistically on the counter. The front page reported a gun massacre at an unaccredited Christian college in the East Bay and, below the fold, a federal crackdown on medical marijuana. I overheard someone talking about his lunch at the Googleplex. "Quinoa cranberry pilaf," I wrote down. And then, "coregasm." Because that was the subsequent topic of discussion: women who have spontaneous orgasms during yoga. The barista was saying how wonderful it was that the issue was receiving attention, coregasms being something a lot of women experienced and were frightened to talk about. Those days were over.

The people of San Francisco were once famous for their refusal of deodorant and unnecessary shearing. Sometimes, walking down the street, past gay construction workers and vibrator stores, I was reminded that this was the place where Harvey Milk was elected (and assassinated), where the bathhouses had flourished (and closed). But most of the time I noticed only that the people of San Francisco appeared to have been suffused with unguents and botanical salves, polished with salts, and scented with the aromatherapeutics sold in the shops that lined Valencia Street. The air smelled of beeswax, lavender, and verbena, when it didn't smell like raw sewage, and the sidewalks in the Mission glittered on sunny days. The food was exquisite. There was a place in Hayes Valley that made liquid-nitrogen ice cream to order. I watched my ice cream magically pressured into existence with a burst of vapor and a pneumatic hiss. This miracle, as the world around me continued apace: moms with Google travel coffee mugs waiting patiently in line, talking about lactation consultants. Online, people had diverted the fear of sin away from coregasms and toward their battles against sugar and flour. "Raw, organic honey, local ghee, and millet chia bread taming my gluten lust," a friend from college announced on social media. "Thank goodness for ancient grains."

At night I was alone, and I would walk down the street hearing sermons in Spanish from the storefront churches and the electronic hum of the BART train below. The city was a dreamworld of glowing screens and analog fetishism, of sex shops and stone fruits. I listened to deranged speeches on buses and street corners by paranoids who connected ancient conspiracies to modern technology. I began to see conspiracies myself. I walked down the sidewalks of the Mission and noted their glittery resemblance to my sparkly powdered blush in its makeup compact. "This sidewalk looks like Super Orgasm," I would think, Super Orgasm being the name of the particular shade of blush I owned. My makeup reveled in contemporary sexual politics: FOR HIM & HER read the sticker on the back of my paraben-free foundation, as if we were all living lives of spontaneity and adventure instead of conformity and punishment. I ran to Golden Gate Park, where giant birds of prey gazed hungrily upon glossy dachshunds. The cyclists passed in shoals, dressed in Google bicycle jerseys.

The idea of free love had a long American tradition of communal experiments, wild-eyed prophets, and jailed heretics. Free love had once meant the right to have sex without procreation; to have sex before marriage; to avoid marriage altogether. It meant freedom of sexual expression for women and gays, and freedom to love across races, genders, and religions. In the twentieth century, post-Freudian idealists believed free love would result in a new politics, even the end of war, and when I heard the phrase "free love" I would helplessly think of 1967, of young people listening to acid rock in this park.

In science fiction, free love had been the future. The new millennium had promised space exploration, fail-safe contraception, cyborg prostitutes, and unrestricted sexuality. But the future had arrived, along with many new freedoms, and free love, as an ideal, had gone out of fashion. We were free to have coregasms, but the hippies had been naive; the science fiction wasn't real. The expansion of sexuality outside of marriage had brought new reasons to trust the traditional controls, reasons such as HIV, the time limits of fertility, the delicacy of feelings. Even as I settled for freedom as an interim state, I planned for my monogamous destiny. My sense of its rightness, after the failed experiments of earlier generations, was like the reconstruction of a baroque national monument that has been destroyed by a bomb. I noticed that it was familiar but not that it was ersatz, or that another kind of freedom had arrived: a blinking cursor in empty space.

The friendly blandness of Google's interface bestowed blessing on the words that passed through its sieve. On Google, all words were created equal, as all ways of choosing to live one's life were equal. Google blurred the distinction between normal and abnormal. The answers its algorithms harvested assured each person of the presence of the like-minded: no one need be alone with her aberrant desires, and no desires were aberrant. The only sexual expectation left to conform to was that love would guide us toward the life we want to live.

What if love failed us? Sexual freedom had now extended to people who never wanted to shake off the old institutions, except to the extent of showing solidarity with friends who did. I had not sought so much choice for myself, and when I found myself with total sexual freedom, I was unhappy.

I decided to visit San Francisco that spring because my desires and my reality had diverged beyond the point of reconciliation. I wanted to picture a different future, one aligned with the freedom of my present, and in those years, San Francisco was where the future was going to be figured out, or at least it was the city America had designated for people who still believed in free love. They sought to unlink the family from a sexual foundation of two people. They believed in intentional communities that could successfully disrupt the monogamous heterosexual tradition. They gave their choices names and they conceived of their actions as social movements. They saw in new technology an opportunity to refashion society, including ideas about sexuality. I understood that the San Franciscans' focus on intention marked the difference between my pessimism and their optimism. When your life does not conform to an idea, and this failure makes you feel bad, throwing away the idea can make you feel better.

I could have found these communities in New York or almost any American city. I would not be the first person to use California as an excuse. I used the West Coast and journalism as alibis and I began to consider my options. Eventually I reached the point where the thought of not having examined the possibilities filled me with dread. But if in my early thirties the future would have simply arrived as I had always imagined, I would have abandoned my inquiry. I would have embraced the project of wifeliness, monogamy, and child-rearing and posted them as triumphs for collective celebration on digital feeds. When I first began to explore the possibilities of free love, I still half-expected that destiny would meet me halfway, that in the middle of all the uncertainty I would come across an exit ramp that would lead me back to all the comfortable expectations and recognizable names.

I was so disingenuous. "But what is your personal journey?" the freethinkers would ask, and I would joke about this later with my friends.

INTERNET DATING

I am not usually comfortable in a bar by myself, but I had been in San Francisco for a week and the apartment I sublet had no chairs in it, just a bed and a couch. My friends in town were married or worked nights. One Tuesday I had lentil soup for supper standing up at the kitchen counter. After I finished, I moved to the couch in the empty living room and sat under the flat overhead light refreshing feeds on my laptop. This was not a way to live. A man would go to a bar alone, I told myself. So I went to a bar alone.

I sat on a stool at the center of the bar, ordered a beer, and refreshed the feeds on my mobile phone. I waited for something to happen. A basketball game played on several monitors at once. The bar had red fake leather booths, Christmas lights, and a female bartender. A lesbian couple cuddled at one end of it. At the other end, around the corner from where I sat, a bespectacled man my age watched the game. As the only man and the only woman alone at the bar, we looked at each other. Then I pretended to watch the game on a monitor that allowed me to look the other way. He turned his back to me to watch the monitor over the pool tables, where the pool players now applauded some exploit.

I waited to be approached. A few stools down, two men broke into laughter. One came over to show me why they were laughing. He handed me his phone and pointed to a Facebook post. I read the post and smiled obligingly. The man returned to his seat. I drank my beer.

I allowed myself a moment's longing for my living room and its couch. The couch had a woolen blanket woven in a Navajo-inspired pattern. There was a cast-iron gas stove in the fireplace. I had fiddled with the knobs and the gas, but couldn't figure out how to ignite it. At night the room had the temperature and pallor of a corpse. There was no television.

I returned to my phone and opened OkCupid, the free Internet dating service. I refreshed the feed that indicated whether other people in the neighborhood were sitting alone in bars. This service was called OkCupid Locals. An OkCupid Locals invitation had to start with the word "Let's":

Let's smoke a joint and hang out ☺
Let's grab a brunch, lunch, beer or some such for some
    friendly Saturday revelry.
Let's get a drink after *Koyaanisqatsi* at the Castro.
Let's meet and tickle.
Let's enjoy a cookie.
Let's become friends and explore somewhere.

I never broadcast an OkCupid chat signal, I just responded. That night I scrolled until I found a handsome man who had written a benign invitation: "Let's get a drink." I looked at his profile.

He was Brazilian. I speak Portuguese. He played the drums. "Tattoos are a big part of my friends' and family's life," he wrote.

I responded to the online beacon, and I went for a drink with a stranger. We kissed, we went back to his place, he showed me his special collection of marijuana plants, and we talked about Brazil. Then I went home and never spoke to him again.

I went on my first Internet date shortly after I bought my first smart phone, in November 2011. Tinder didn't yet exist, and in New York my friends used OkCupid, so that's where I signed up. I also signed up to Match, but OkCupid was the one I favored, mostly because I got such constant and overwhelming attention from men there. The square-jawed bankers who reigned over Match, with their pictures of scuba diving in Bali and skiing in Aspen, paid me so little attention it made me feel sorry for myself. The low point came when I sent a digital wink to a man whose profile read, "I have a dimple on my chin," and included photos of him playing rugby and standing bare-chested on a deep-sea fishing vessel holding a mahi-mahi the size of a tricycle. He didn't respond to my wink.

I joined OkCupid with the pseudonym "viewfromspace." In the "About" section of my profile I wrote, "I like watching nature documentaries and eating pastries." I answered all the questions indicating an interest in casual sex in the negative. I wanted a boyfriend. I was also badly hung up on my last boyfriend and wanted to stop thinking about him. Many people on the site had this problem. People cheerily listed their favorite movies and hoped for the best, but darkness simmered beneath the chirpy surface. An extensive accrual of regrets lurked behind even the most well-adjusted profile. I read *The Red and the Black* to remind myself that sunny equanimity in the aftermath of heartbreak was not always the order of the day. On the other hand, I liked that on the dating sites people hit on each other with no ambiguity of intention. A gradation of subtlety, sure: from the basic "You're cute," to the off-putting "Hi there, would you like to come over, smoke a joint and let me take nude photos of you in my living room?"

I found the algorithms put me in the same area—social class and level of education—as the people I went on dates with, but otherwise did very little to predict whom I would like. I seemed to attract, in both online and real-life dating, a statistically anomalous number of vegetarians. I am not a vegetarian.

I went on a date with a composer who invited me to a John Cage concert at Juilliard. After the concert we looked for the bust of Béla Bartók on Fifty-seventh Street. We couldn't find it, but he told me how Bartók had died there of leukemia. We talked about college, and the poetry of Wallace Stevens. We both liked the novels of Thomas Pynchon. We had all this in common but I wished I were somewhere else. As we drank beers in an Irish pub in Midtown, I could think of five or ten people with whom I would have rather spent the evening drinking beers. But the object, now, was to find a boyfriend, and none of the many people I already knew were possible boyfriends.

For our second date we went out for ramen in the East Village. I ended the night early, on the way out lamenting what a long day it had been. He next invited me to a concert at Columbia and then to dinner at his house. I said yes but canceled at the last minute, claiming illness and adding that I thought our dating had run its course.

I had hurt his feelings. My cancellation, he wrote, had cost him a "ton of time shopping, cleaning and cooking that I didn't really have to spare in the first place a few days before a deadline . . ."

He punctuated almost exclusively with Pynchonian ellipses. I apologized, then stopped responding. In the months that followed he continued to write long e-mails with updates of his life, and I continued not responding until it was as if he were lobbing his sadness into a black hole, where I absorbed it into my own sadness.

I went on a date with a furniture craftsman. We met at a coffee shop. It was a sunny afternoon in late February, but a strange snowfall began after we arrived, the flakes sparkling in the sun. The coffee shop was belowground, and we sat at a table by a window that put us just below two chihuahuas tied to a bench on the sidewalk outside. They shivered uncontrollably despite their fitted jackets. They looked down at us through the window, chewing on their leashes. The woodworker bought me a coffee and drank tea in a pint glass.

He showed me photos of furniture he made. He had callused hands and was tall. He was attractive but his blue eyes shifted restlessly around the room and he looked bored. We discovered we had been born in the same hospital, Allentown Hospital in Allentown, Pennsylvania, except that I was seven months older. In another era, the era when marriage was dictated by religion, family, and the village, we might have had several children by now. Instead my parents had moved halfway across the country when I was three years old, he had stayed in Allentown until adulthood, and now we both lived in Bedford-Stuyvesant, Brooklyn, and were thirty. He thought of himself as defiant, and loved being a craftsman only as much as he had hated working in an office. After drinking his tea, he went to the bathroom, came back, and wordlessly put on his coat. I stood up and did the same. We walked up the stairs into the February wind. We said goodbye.

I went on a date with a man who turned out to be a hairstylist. "A nod and a bow, Ms. Space," he had written. He arrived late to our appointment in Alphabet City, having accommodated some last-minute clients who wanted unscheduled blow-drying for their own dates. On either side of his neck he had tattoos of crossed scimitars. I asked him what the tattoos meant. He said they meant nothing. They were mistakes. He pushed up his sleeves and revealed more mistakes. As a teenager in Dallas he had let his friends use him as a training canvas. To call the tattoos mistakes was different from regretting them. He didn't regret them. He said it was just that his sixteen-year-old self was giving him the finger. "You think you've changed," the sixteen-year-old version of him was saying through the tattoos: "Fuck you, I'm still here."

None of the careful self-presentation in the OkCupid profiles ever revealed what I would discover within several minutes of meeting a person: that I never seemed to want to have sex with anybody I met online. In real life, casual sex was straightforward. I would meet someone at a party. One of us would ask the other out. Then we would have a date or two and have sex, even when we knew we weren't in love and the relationship wouldn't "go anywhere." Sometimes we would skip the dating part. I told myself that my celibacy on OkCupid was because I thought of Internet dating as a "project" I was undertaking, where I would apply a "seriousness" that was absent from my actual social life. I had an idea about "standards" that had to be met before I would consider having sex. The truth was that when I met with these men, most of whom superseded my "standards," nothing stirred in my body. I felt that it was usually clear, to both parties, that while we could have had sex it would have been more out of resignation and duty than real desire. If Internet dating made me feel like I was taking control of my life in some way, having sex with people I didn't really desire would just remind me of the futility of trying to engineer a relationship into existence. Sex, when it was the result of an accumulation of energy between me and another person, really did make me feel better, but to pretend that feeling was there when it wasn't was more dispiriting than going home alone.

The body, I started to learn, was not a secondary entity. The mind contained very few truths that the body withheld. There was little of import in an encounter between two bodies that would fail to be revealed rather quickly. The epistolary run-up to the date only rarely revealed the truth of a man's good humor or introversion, his anxiety or social grace. Until the bodies were introduced, seduction was only provisional. I began responding only to people with very short profiles, then began forgoing the profiles altogether, using them only to see that people on OkCupid Locals knew how to spell and didn't have rabidly right-wing politics.

Still, I avoided any mention of sex in my profile. I also avoided all men who led with explicitly sexual overtures. My avoidance of any overt reference to sex meant that Internet dating was like standing in a room full of people recommending restaurants to one another without describing the food. No, it was worse than that. It was a room full of hungry people who instead discussed the weather. If a person offered me a watermelon, I would reject him for not having an umbrella. The right to avoid the subject of sex was structurally embedded in the most popular dating sites. They had been designed that way, because otherwise women would not have used them.

The man generally held responsible for Internet dating as we know it today is a native of Illinois called Gary Kremen. In 1992, Kremen was a twenty-nine-year-old computer scientist and one of the many graduates of Stanford Business School running software companies in the Bay Area. After a childhood as a pudgy Jewish misfit in Skokie, Kremen had decided upon two goals for his adult life: he wanted to get married and he wanted to earn money. In pursuit of marriage, he went on lots of dates. He soon developed a habit of calling 1-900 numbers—not the phone-sex kind, but the kind that were listed with classified personal ads in the newspaper. As a standard practice at the time, newspapers charged readers two dollars a minute to leave a voice-mail response to a personal ad. Kremen had run up a lot of bills by making such calls. He was, in his own words, "kind of a loser." One afternoon at work at his software company Kremen had an idea: what if he had a database of all the single women in the world?

Kremen and four male partners formed Electric Classifieds Inc., a business premised on the idea of re-creating on the Web the classifieds section of newspapers, beginning with the personals. They found an office in a basement in the South Park neighborhood of San Francisco and registered a domain name, Match.com.

"ROMANCE—LOVE—SEX—MARRIAGE AND RELATIONSHIPS," read the headline on an early business plan Electric Classifieds presented to potential investors. "American business has long understood that people knock the doors down for dignified and effective services that fulfill these most powerful human needs." In deference to his investors, Kremen eventually removed "sex" from his list of needs.

Many of the basic parts of most online dating sites were laid out in this early document. Subscribers completed a questionnaire, indicating the kind of relationship they wanted—"marriage partner, steady date, golf partner, or travel companion." Users posted photos: "A customer could choose to show himself in various favorite activities and clothing to give the viewing customer a stronger sense of personality and physical character." The business plan cited a market forecast that suggested 50 percent of the adult population would be single by 2000. By 2008, 48 percent of American adults were unmarried, compared with 28 percent in 1960.

Electronic Classifieds suggested that "many people feel freer when talking electronically than they do face to face." Kremen drew on the experience of early Internet chat rooms and bulletin boards, which one newspaper article from the time described as "an antiseptic version of a 70s singles bar." Online, "people who meet in crowded chat rooms often create their own private chat rooms where they engage in cybersex—the keyboard equivalent of phone sex." But the Internet was most prevalent in sectors that had historically excluded women—the military, finance, mathematics, and engineering—and the new World Wide Web and its online predecessors had acquired a sexist reputation. "The brave new interactive world is still a club for white male members," lamented a 1993 manual called *The Joy of Cybersex*. "It is by no means politically correct."

Knowing that a successful heterosexual dating site had to have roughly equal numbers of women and men subscribers, Kremen hired a team of women marketers led by a former Stanford classmate named Fran Maier. Maier learned that women were more likely to use the site if it emphasized traditional dating rituals and presented sex as a secondary question. If the Internet chat rooms were the equivalent of online singles bars, Match, Maier said, would be like "a very nice restaurant or exclusive club." The company forbade sexually explicit content and photographs. They modified the questionnaire to include questions about children and religion to emphasize that while any kind of encounter could be had through Match, the site would favor the impression of being a place for people who were looking for lasting relationships. They published editorial content about courtship, as in a dating column about how to use emoticons to "e-flirt," and offered guidelines about safety, suggesting that women arrange their dates at public places and not give out their addresses to strangers. They banned any mention of biological clocks, which might have made the site look like a place for desperate people. They gave the interface a clean, white background and a heart-shaped logo. All of this was for women; recruiting men had never been a problem.

Match set a template for the industry, which grew as the World Wide Web did. As the databases multiplied, they became more specific, tailored to ethnicities and religions. Then came the era of matchmaking science and algorithms, then Internet dating for free, and finally the era of the mobile phone. Each dating technology looking to attract an equal number of women and men, no matter the business strategy, had to ensure that a woman could join the site without having to make any sexual declarations. The more an Internet dating site or application led with the traditional signifiers of masculine heterosexual desire—photographs of lingerie-clad women, open hints about casual sex—the less likely women were to sign up for it. When hackers stole user data from the website Ashley Madison (tag line: "Life is short. Have an affair.") they revealed that only 14 percent of user records belonged to women, half the percentage that had been advertised by the company's founder. Of this number, thousands of profiles appeared to be female "bots" programmed to send automated messages to men.

The Internet dating business was the place where I first encountered a popular marketing concept called "the clean, well-lighted place." This phrase, divorced completely from its origins as the title of an Ernest Hemingway story set in a bar in Spain, came up often when businesspeople spoke about creating a "woman-friendly environment" for sexuality. Cleaning and lighting a place usually meant the removal of pornographic or sexually explicit imagery. "A clean, well-lighted place" was the motto of the pioneering feminist sex-toy shop Good Vibrations in San Francisco, which had taken vibrators and dildos from their porn-laden packages and placed them in denuded simplicity like art objects on pedestals. At first the idea had stood for a reclamation of sexuality, an aphoristic amulet against the lingering specter of 1970s movie houses, hot tubs, singles bars, and abused porn stars on quaaludes, but the concept applied equally well to the age of unsolicited dick pics and "Meet hot singles in your area who want to fuck you now!" In online dating, the clean, well-lighted place meant a sex-free environment in which to consider people with whom one might eventually have sex. For some women, even acknowledging that they were on OkCupid with any sort of intention, let alone a sexual one, was undesirable, so it benefited the dating sites to be as anodyne and blandly enthusiastic as possible. Sam Yagan, one of OkCupid's founders, told me that one of the unexpected advantages of being free was that the service allowed women to tell themselves that they were not actually looking for a date. "Like, they'll be, like, 'Oh, I just met a boyfriend on OkCupid. I didn't even sign up for dating!' Okay. You're right." Yagan rolled his eyes. "Literally about a third of the success e-mails we get from women have a disclaimer in them that says 'I didn't sign up for dating.'" And success, of course, was defined as love. According to another OkCupid founder, Christian Rudder, the numbers of heterosexual women who explicitly stated they were on the site for casual sex was disproportionately low, only 0.8 percent, compared with 6.1 percent of straight men, 6.9 percent of gay men, and 7 percent of gay women.

The business strategy was different on websites that excluded women. The founders of Manhunt, which transitioned from a phone chat line to a website in 2001 and became one of the most popular early dating sites for gay men, quickly recognized that in the world of men interested in meeting men, what job the person had or where he went to college were secondary questions. Sexual attraction and explicitly sexual communication tended to come first.

"A website operated by straight people just does not register with gay men," Jonathan Crutchley, Manhunt's co-founder, said in a 2007 interview. "When you fill out their questionnaires the questions that a woman would ask a man when she's looking for someone to marry, like 'How much money do you make?' 'Do you want children?'—these are ridiculous questions. A gay man could not care less how much money you make, could not care less about wanting children. They want to know your physical attributes; they want to see pictures; they want to know what you're into." It was not that his clients did not seek long-term partnerships and families, said Crutchley. Many of them did. The difference between the two approaches was in the process of evaluation. For a significant number of men, sex had its own intrinsic value and quantitative metrics, independent of the qualifications that determined whether you wanted to live with someone and adopt babies with him. Sexual attraction was not a mysterious chemical accident but something that could be researched and described in language. Sexual desires were not ineffable wisps of the imagination; they could be named. Someone like me, in contrast, believed that if I enjoyed going to a museum with a man the sexual attraction would just follow, without anybody having to talk about it.

In March 2009, a "social discovery" app called Grindr invited men to "find gay, bi, and curious guys for free near you!" When enabled on a mobile device, Grindr produced a grid of users, organized in order of proximity. Information about each user ranged from a headless torso with a sobriquet, to smiling, fully clothed portraits with real first names. Full nudity was not allowed in profile pictures, in part to comply with the rules of the app stores, but people could send each other more explicit photos once they began chatting. Grindr's founder, a thirty-two-year-old New Yorker named Joel Simkhai, said that the app was more about accessing a social community than it was about finding sex. He had invented it because he wanted to know who around him was gay, and 67 percent of users said they used it to make friends. On the other hand, it was called Grindr. *The New York Times* kept describing it as a "hookup app." The logic, I guess, was that a conversation that began with "R u hung?" had as its end goal an anonymous sexual encounter, whereas one that began with "Hey there gorgeous, ready for the weekend?" would result in a malted with two straws in it followed by an engagement ring. I think that was the story we were telling ourselves.

Before Grindr presented another idea about how to use an iPhone, Internet dating had succeeded as a technological change that did not dismantle certain myths about the progression of romance. OkCupid was just another way to ask someone out on a date. Grindr introduced the theory that one could look at a picture of someone's abdomen and soon be having sex with a neighbor, and the theory became a question. Should one do this? My answer was no, obviously not. I could only see threats of sexual violence and disease. Still, I liked the idea of it, I liked that our phones beamed signals to orbiting satellites to reveal people only a few feet away; I liked the idea that the strangers of the city could lower the barriers of their isolation. I anticipated when such a technology would become available for my demographic even though I already knew I wouldn't be bold enough to act on its potential. I wasn't alone in wanting it to happen. Web articles speculated about the arrival of a "Grindr for straight people" or a "Grindr for lesbians." These articles had a wistful tone, and even the ones that fretted over "hookup culture" believed in the power of a

GPS-equipped mobile device to sexually liberate women, as if the technology would free us from all the fears and superstitions. The consternation about the "decline of romance" revealed inadvertent optimism that we really could become a society where every single person would feel sexual belonging by activating a program on her phone on a Friday night. Even the opprobrium was idealistic, with its faith that technology would change everything.

In 2011, Simkhai launched such an app. He called it Blendr, but it failed to deliver results comparable to its men-seeking-men counterpart. Once he allowed everyone into the network, it lost its purpose as a means by which to find a coherent social community. Worse, when users started chatting on Blendr and a man sent an unsolicited picture of his penis, women deleted the app.

Tinder arrived a year later. It was a general-interest dating app that in many ways mimicked the interface of Grindr. It showed photos of other users in a person's immediate vicinity with only name, age, and a tag line of written text. Depending on your feelings for these people, you swiped them to the left (no) or right (yes). It was a Grindr for straight people, but its success with straight people had everything to do with changing Grindr into a clean, well-lighted space. Tinder had innocuous graphic design and peppy animation. The copy of its messaging was buoyant with exclamation points. The profiles were tied to Facebook profiles so that you knew a person was "real." Users could not exchange photographs within the app, to lower the risk of unwanted sexual imagery. They could exchange messages only when two people swiped each other to the right and would "match." Tinder's founders called this the "double opt in." The founders of Tinder denied any comparisons with Grindr, or that the app's purpose was to help people arrange casual sex. "Girls aren't wired that way," said Sean Rad, adding that married people could also use it "to find tennis partners."

I didn't think straight women lived dramatically different lives from gay men. I saw two cultures with distinct stories about the right way to act and to be, with differences in what they were willing to declare about themselves. Grindr had presented an idea. Tinder had modified that idea according to another culture's concepts of propriety. The gestures toward the two mythologies were very banal: a black screen background versus a white one; photos of body parts versus photos of people doing adventure sports. Two sets of symbols and gestures that would end the same way, with two people in a room together and no guidance.

Of course I knew many friends who had fallen in love online, who had found in the technology a clear, sense-making corridor from being single to being in a couple with no detours into other possibilities. I felt more affinity with the people who had not found love, especially those who expressed a feeling that endless stretches of Internet dating put them outside of an ontological monoculture that they could neither describe nor name: people who had gone for several years without bringing anybody home for family holidays, who were used to going to weddings by themselves, who knew they embodied some ahistorical demographic whose numbers were now significant but which was lacking any sense of group consciousness, let alone any declaration of sexual purpose.

These technologies, which presented a certain possibility of freedom, revealed how little we demanded. In theory, I could behave as I wished. Without breaking any laws I could dress as a nun and get spanked by a person dressed as the pope. I could watch a porn starlet hula-hoop on my computer while I had sex with a battery-operated prosthetic. I could contact a stranger on the

Internet, tell him to meet me at the north entrance of the Wool-
worth Building, tell him I would make myself known only if he
arrived carrying three Mylar balloons referencing distinct Dis-
ney animated classics, and then, if he fulfilled my wishes, go to
his place for sex. I could do all these things without having to wear
a scarlet letter, get thrown in jail, or be stoned in public.

I did not do any of these things. My timidity not only concerned ideas of sexual "safety" (especially since most such ideas
were ruses that gave women a false sense of control in an unpre-
dictably violent world). My avoidance of sex also had a lot to do
with an equation, a relationship of exchange around which I organized my ideas. I saw sex as a lever that moderated climatic
conditions within the chamber of life, with a negative correla-
tion between the number of people I slept with and the likelihood of encountering love. Being sexually cautious meant I was
looking for "something serious." Having sex with more people
meant I privileged the whims of the instant over transcendent
higher-order commitments that developed over long stretches
of time. I equated promiscuity with youth culture and thought of
longer monogamous relationships as more adult, and it seemed
depressing to still be having casual sex on a regular basis for an
interminable number of years. The arbitrary nature of these cor-
relations had not occurred to me.

Even though I felt certain I would eventually meet someone,
I consumed many theories about why I was alone. The books
and magazines I read supplied an ongoing and detailed investi-
gation of female malaise. All over America women wondered what
had happened to the adult life they had imagined as children, and
whether to blame its elusiveness on material changes or personal
shortcomings. The old-fashioned theory that a woman might be
unlucky and had not met the "right guy" no longer satisfied them.
Books urged the single woman to "settle" and marry the imper-

fect suitor, or to accept that "he's just not that into you." The literature counseled behavior modification, telling her to follow
"the rules" or to temper adoration because "men love bitches."
Another set of ideas reassured the woman that she was not to
blame—her problems were caused by the Internet: porn had encouraged a culture of loveless, aggressive sexuality or had drained
men of sexual animus; the "marketplace" of Internet dating made
consumer products of humans and overwhelmed them with
choices. Fake-sociology journalists explained to her that she lived
in an unfortunate era of societal confusion caused by unclear
postfeminist gender roles. This literature could be helpful. It recognized a situation. But it never found a way out.

Instead, these theories compressed the life of "woman today"
into a single, unhappy narrative. It began with accounts of how
technology was ruining things in high school, how teenage girls
had now assimilated ejaculate in the face and Brazilian bikini
waxes, how blow jobs were the new kissing, and how girls used
social media to send boys pictures of their breasts to be popular.
These young women would progress to college, where, after initially thinking that having sex with a man meant committed
monogamy, a woman would first suffer disappointment then
shift her outlook to "try not to get attached." Absent the intention
of finding love as she pursued sex, the story went, love would
never arrive for her. The young woman would then arrive in New
York or Dallas or Chicago, where men don't pay for dinner anymore, and romance is only so many text messages sent while drunk
at two a.m. The men were listless dilettantes, the women gym-
toned and frantically successful. The confused heroine was often
counseled to withhold sex, in exchange for what wasn't exactly
clear. As she aged, the articles shifted to stories of regret, how at
one point she thought that marrying young would be detrimental
to her career, and now she worried about her attractiveness and

fertility, as if every woman is presented with a clear choice between career and family in her mid-to-late twenties. By the age of forty the single women, tired of waiting for commitment from men, were using technology to get pregnant by themselves. Babies equaled the fulfillment of a great destiny, although women who had married and had children sounded extremely busy and unhappy, suffered in their careers, and lost interest in sex. The narrative of married life culminated in a hazy binary of male politicians who cheated on their middle-aged wives versus happy couples who settled into gardening, fitness, and conversation about television shows over dinner. Researchers were hard at work trying to invent a pill to incite sexual desire for married women who loved their husbands but did not love having sex with them.

The stories all became one story, documenting a long series of contemporary threats to the ideal of "the committed monogamous relationship," that managed to include every expression of female sexuality that happened outside of it. The only way a woman could keep from undermining this version of love was by saying no to sex, never pandering to male desire, and never expressing any overt sexual interest in the new channels of photography and text. Critics would lament that if a person were to design a fantasy world based on the whims of a young man, its rules and ethics would look much like the social world of the contemporary college campus. What men wanted from sex was assumed to be sex; what women were described as wanting when it came to sex was not sex at all, but rather a relationship in which one had sex, a structure in which sex happened. The consensus about what young men were said to want from sex—lots of it, perhaps with a number of different partners—had no female corollary. "What kind of sex do you like?" was a question the Internet dating apps did not ask.

If a woman thought she would most likely sabotage her future happiness through her sexual choices, it followed that it would be difficult to plainly state one's desires, or even to describe in explicit language the sex she wanted to have. Every sexual expression raised the question of false consciousness: women were described as "objectifying themselves," "degrading themselves," or "submitting unthinkingly to contemporary pressures." They were accused of succumbing to "the pornification of society" and altering their bodies to please men. Rather than following the natural impulse of an adventurous young person a woman was "adopting the sexual behavior of the most opportunistic guy on campus" or "masquerading her desperation as freedom." Once married, a woman who became a swinger was accommodating the desires of her philandering partner rather than acting on her own free will. A woman could not even give a blow job without a voice in the back of her head suggesting she had been "used."

I saw that it was taken for granted, or asserted by books of biological determinism such as Louann Brizendine's *The Female Brain*, that the monogamous relationship made women the most happy, was where they most enjoyed sex, and that this sort of commitment brought women both freedom and security. This line of thinking forced me into a gendered role that I resented. If every expression of free sexuality by a woman would be second-guessed, it left men as the sole rational agents of sexual narrative. The woman was rarely granted the heroic role of seducer. If a woman pursued a strictly sexual experience, she was seen as succumbing to the wishes of the sovereign subject. If the sex she had with no commitments made her unhappy, it was not simply bad sex but rather proof of her delusion that it could be good. Male sexual desire was the overwhelming constant, the chemical imperative, and female desire either a concession or a taming influence, whose achievement was not in the act of seduction but in wresting a man's interest from the wider field to her alone. What a stupid way to live, where the pure force of sexual desire could never be trusted. Casual sex, abundant and plentifully available to any woman willing to announce her interest in having it, always came second to this precious and rare thing, the loving relationship. Very few people questioned the worth or desirability of this denouement. I didn't question it either.

It was the very naturalness of the committed relationship, its supposed inevitability, the ne plus ultra of comfort and respect that it represented, that induced the worst mania in the women I knew, because many of us felt simultaneously entitled to it as a destiny while also finding it impossible to achieve, what with our technology, our moral landscape, and our lack of clear gender roles. Unlike school or work, the amount of effort and thought we put into it had no correlative result, because the outcome depended on the behavior and complicity of another kind of person. "It is agonizing for a woman to assume responsibility for her own life," wrote Simone de Beauvoir in *The Second Sex*, first published in 1949. Many decades later this was still true: to give up on the *idea* of the relationship would be to assume a mantle of preternatural self-sufficiency. Letting go of the ideal relationship, to instead declare herself autonomous, to treat sexual desire as a force that gave life meaning rather than as a means to a structural end, would run counter to the thing that most religions and every happy ending she had ever seen assured a woman would bring her the most joy.

Even if I rejected the books and magazine articles, which forecasted a range of consequences from the simple decision to have sex or not, they colonized my mind. Experience indicated that love would not be more likely to arrive if I rejected sex, but I read articles that spoke of a woman's "choice" between casual sex and serious relationships. I learned about an "economic" theory of sex, wherein if women make sex more readily available (never mind wanting it) its "price" drops, and men have to "do less" to get it. "She struggles with him in the effort to uphold her independence, and she battles with the rest of the world to preserve the 'situation' that dooms her to dependence," wrote Beauvoir. "This double game is difficult to play, explaining in part the disturbed and nervous state in which many women spend their lives."

I had a friend who began pursuing casual sex as a declared intention in her twenties, when she lived in New York. In New York, her strategy had not been complicated: when her friends left the bar, she would stay. When she later moved to a smaller city, the bars closed earlier. A car-bound transportation system meant people drank less. She turned to the Internet.

While plenty of men offered themselves as interested in casual sex on OkCupid, too many encounters ended sadly: it was, after all, a dating website, and she did not want to talk about feelings, she wanted to have intense, satisfying sexual encounters. She began using the "Casual Encounters" classifieds on Craigslist. She would go on at night and respond to ads. She had a system: first, an exchange of photos. Then a phone call. She is deft and decisive, and these traits gave her an advantage when it came to casual sex. Every phone call, she would lay out a list of rules. She would get a real name. She would say that everything they did would be consensual and that if she said "no" or wanted to stop that all sex would stop. They would use condoms. If she liked the man, and he agreed to her conditions, she would go to his place. She would meet him outside and then they would go in and have sex. She understood all of the risks.

Sometimes the encounters would be depressing, but even the

worst ones would give her stories to tell. When the encounters went well they could be powerful sexual experiences. Some of the men who used Craigslist to seek out casual sex, she said, were really good at sex. They were people for whom sex was an end in itself, who had a lot of experience, who tended to have an ardent fascination with and interest in the body and in pleasure.

When I spoke to her about it, she was now in her thirties, and more interested in having a monogamous relationship. I asked her what her Internet sex experiences had given her. The most important thing, she said, was learning that if she overtly expressed interest in having noncommittal sex with men who also seemed interested in sex, they almost always responded positively. They would delight in her willingness and affirm how much they desired her. This affirmation was not, as perhaps she had been led to believe, "cheap" for being readily available. (Or rather, as another friend once put it: "Yeah, it's cheap—it's free!") She learned that even if she never found love, she would always find someone who would want to have sex. It made her feel good about herself and her body, it made her more confident, she grew in her awareness of her own agency and had more control than she was used to experiencing in the confines of the traditional view of dating, where the idea remained that sex was to be withheld until some indication of emotional commitment was revealed. When a woman wanted casual sex, and not a boyfriend, the old gender roles were often reversed. She was the one who could choose; she was the one to whom men would clamor to reply. These lessons outweighed what she saw as the downsides: the depressing encounters that were really depressing, the fact that her partners in the future would have to reckon with the extent of her sexual history, the risks. Also, she said happily, "now I'm really good at sex." By which she meant, I supposed, that she had overcome the idea of good sex as a chemical accident, as rare as falling in love.

I never felt secure enough to pursue sex online. In the depths of loneliness, however, Internet dating provided me with a lot of opportunities to go to a bar and have a drink with a stranger on nights that would otherwise have been spent unhappy and alone. I met all kinds of people: an X-ray technician, a green tech entre-preneur, a computer programmer with whom I enjoyed a chaste fondness over the course of several weeks. We were both shy and my feelings were tepid (as, I gathered, were his), but we went to the beach, he told me all about mushroom foraging, he ordered his vegetarian burritos in Spanish, and we shared many mutual dislikes.

Internet dating had evolved to present the world around us, the people in our immediate vicinity, and to fulfill the desires of a particular moment. At no point did it offer guidance in what to do with such a vast array of possibility. While the lonely might harbor a secret object, from the desire for a brief sexual encounter to a longing for love, the technology itself promised nothing. It brought us people, but it did not tell us what to do with them.

ORGASMIC MEDITATION

The organization OneTaste was careful about the impressions it gave, since its mission to "bring female orgasm to the world" could sometimes be misinterpreted. Once a week, OneTaste therefore offered an open house, where curious members of the public could meet practitioners of what the organization called orgasmic meditation, or OM-ing, in a casual and friendly setting, without any of the actual orgasms or meditating. Advertised as "A room of people (cool, fun people) engaged in honest, humorous, playful conversation around topics we mostly only consider having in our head," the meetings were held every Wednesday evening at OneTaste's small headquarters on Moss Street, a secluded back alley in San Francisco's South of Market district. The building was a squat two-story former warehouse, its exterior painted a neutral gray, its front a façade of frosted glass windows. A velvet curtain shielded the front door from the view of the street, and entrances were monitored by beaming members of the organization, who greeted newcomers with the confidence and searching eye contact characteristic of all purveyors of conversion experiences.

I entered here one evening, gave my name to one of a small fleet of enthusiastic people presiding over clipboards, and walked from the foyer into OneTaste's inner chamber, a clean, skylit space with polished concrete floors and exposed wooden beams. In one corner was a table holding coffee and tea. Music played softly through speakers. Two rows of chairs were placed in a half circle; in front of them another row, of fabric chairs lined up on the floor. Maybe twenty or so people occupied these seats, a healthy-looking, multicultural group of people who mostly appeared to be in their thirties or forties.

I sat on the end of the back row of chairs, and said hello to the woman sitting next to me. Her name was Melissa. She was originally from Kansas City but had most recently been living in New York. She had only just moved to San Francisco. She worked in public relations. She was white, had long brown hair and a full figure, and wore a knit dress. Her looks and dress would have been visually congruent in a vast array of settings: she would not have stuck out at a church in Kansas City, or in a bar in Midtown Manhattan, or at a Whole Foods in Austin, or on a back patio in Atlanta, and nor did she stick out in an orgasmic meditation information session in San Francisco. We compared New York and San Francisco, agreeing that the latter's slower pace and manageable size had its advantages. We talked about how expensive the taxis were. We ran out of things to talk about. Melissa had been to OneTaste before. "Everyone is really nice here," she finally said, and it was true.

In front of her, a slim man with light brown skin and glasses turned around and stared at us. He and the man next to him said something to Melissa and she listened. "You don't want women and women sitting together?" she said. So she stood up and switched spots with the man, who now sat next to me. Still staring, in the friendly, focused, interested way that indicated to me he had clearly had some experience in this setting, he introduced himself as Marcus. We shook hands. Meanwhile, the music that had been playing was turned down. A man and a woman sat down on stools before the half circle, and a quiet settled over the room.

The man and woman did not immediately speak. Instead they gazed thoughtfully around the room with tranquil, wise glances. They were both attractive, and radiated the clean healthy blondness endemic to Northern Californians. They were casually dressed. He was in his late twenties, sandy-headed, clean-shaven and with symmetrical features, the sleeves of his faded T-shirt nicely taut against his biceps. He had the human neutrality of an Apple store or IKEA—if he had been a piece of furniture he would have been a solid but elegant construction of blond wood. Both wore jeans, hers with a plaid pearl-buttoned shirt of thin cotton that allowed the edges of the tattoos that framed her chest to peek through at the collar. Her nails were a vivid tomato red and her wavy blond hair delicately tousled. I could picture her leaning against a vintage pickup truck in a field of wheat at the golden hour, perhaps in an advertisement.

His name was Eli; hers was Alisha. He had been OM-ing for three and a half years; she had been practicing for more than six. They told us this now, and then explained the meeting we were attending as a way to introduce the practice to us, the public. We would begin, they said, by playing a series of three games to get to know one another, and then they would explain the practice of orgasmic meditation for those who were unfamiliar with it.

The first game was called One Mind. To play it, we answered a single question with rapid responses made sequentially around the circle. First we gave our names. The next question was "Why did you come here?" I was one of several people who answered "curiosity." Already, however, people showed an apparent eagerness to make their answers sexual, although Eli and Alisha had yet to indicate that OneTaste had anything to do with sex, per se. The third question confirmed that the intention of the whole endeavor was to in fact encourage us to talk about sex in an overt way. It was "What does your red hot desire look like?"

The responses ranged from "Being tied in a bed," to "Naked in a forest in Tahoe," to "Giving head for fifteen minutes straight." One woman said, "I can't fathom it so I'm here to figure that out." Someone else gave a sylvan vision of a fawn caught in a sunbeam in a tree-filled glen. A man in his mid-fifties whose hair seemed styled into a monk's tonsure said only, "I'm available." Someone else said, "Licking pussies." Another, to Alisha: "You, when you're turned inside out." The familiarity and gusto with which many people in the room played the games indicated that they already knew one another. They emphasized their ease and comfort with discussing sex to galvanize the rest into adopting the same attitude.

We proceeded to the second game, called Hot Seat. For this game a volunteer sat on the stool in front of the room, the aforementioned hot seat, and answered questions from the audi ence. The questions were supposed to be "interested rather than interesting"—oriented to show curiosity toward the recipient and not to make a provocative point. The game's rules forbade any rejoinder beyond "thank you." If the answer satisfied the questioner before the person in the hot seat had finished responding, he or she could cut off the response with "thank you."

"Who wants to be in the hot seat?" asked Eli. At least a dozen hands shot up, including that of Melissa from Kansas City. The moderators chose a small, dark-haired woman named Rebecca, with whom they seemed to be friends. "Rebecca, you're glowing," said Eli. She did appear to be glowing. She sat down and awaited her first question.

"Rebecca, why are you glowing?" someone finally asked.

"Because I found my orgasm tonight," she answered.

"Thank you."

Rebecca pointed to the next questioner.

"Where was it?"

"My entire body."

"Thank you."

Another woman sat in the hot seat. The questions continued: "Are men who want to date you intimidated by you?" asked one. "I don't know," she said. Further questions revealed that the hot seater was actually in love with a woman, so later someone asked, "How did it make you feel when you were asked that question about dating men?"

A lanky man with harem pants, blue eyes, and an indeterminate northern European accent took to the stool.

"Are you German?"

"No."

"Thank you."

"How did you hear about OneTaste?"

"Someone told me about it at a party."

"Thank you."

He said he was happy to have come because these were the kinds of things he always wanted to talk about.

"What sort of things?"

"Sensual things."

"Thank you."

"What do you hope will happen?"

"I hope to meet people and maybe have sex with one."

"Thank you."

A woman named Lisa sat in the hot seat. She pointed at a man with his hand upraised.

"Jose," she said, calling him by name.

"What are you frustrated about?" he asked.

"Jose," she answered.

"Thank you," said Jose.

"Why are you frustrated with Jose?" asked someone else.

"Because I want to fuck him."

Everybody laughed.

"Thank you."

Finally the moderators called on Melissa. She had looked happy, but once she was sitting in the hot seat she began to cry.

"Why are you crying?" someone asked.

"I don't know," she said.

"Thank you."

She did not seem to be crying from despair. Rather, the idea was that she cried like someone who has been unhappy for a long time, has unexpectedly found solace, and now can hardly conceive of the darkness to which she had previously confined herself.

We proceeded to the third and final game: Intimacies. Alisha explained that it was Intimacies that had made her realize, when she had first encountered OneTaste, that she had found somewhere she belonged. The rules of the game held that people directly addressed other people's "turn-ons": we went around in a circle, and each person was allowed to make a statement to another person directly, or the group at large. A man named Rajiv told the woman named Lisa that he was attracted to her. When the game reached her she addressed him, "Let's talk." Somebody told the not-German man he had "turned her on." Another man addressed all of the women in the group, expressing relief to hear them talking about their desires. Another liked someone's glasses. One man from across the room said to a woman on the floor with blond curly hair, "You're not normally the kind of person I'm attracted to but you really turn me on." Another: "When I saw you kissing someone earlier in the kitchen I felt disappointed." Each of these statements was to be met only with a simple "thank you."

A lot of people addressed Melissa, whose tears had acted as an invitation to the more shy people in the group. When my turn came I told Melissa that the contrast between our shallow small talk and her tears reminded me how much is going on beneath every banal conversation. Much of the attention also focused on a small man dressed all in white sitting on the floor. He was pale and seemed to radiate illness and depression. At one prompt he had referred to the end of a relationship. In Intimacies several people addressed him. One told him that he looked troubled. Another said that he was surprised to see him back for the second time. The sallow man in white used his chance to share an intimacy to thank the friends who had accompanied him. Marcus, the man who had been staring at the beginning, addressed me: he had been watching me during the evening, he said, and would see me shut down, and then at other times open up and light up. "Thank you," I said, annoyed.

After the "games" finished, Alisha and Eli launched into a brief explanation of what orgasmic meditation actually is. Orgasmic meditation, or OM, is a fifteen-minute practice between a woman and a partner. The word choice—*practice*—deliberately recalled yoga and meditation. For the OM-ers it implied an ongoing, daily ritual in which one gained incremental expertise and wisdom over time.

A couple begins an orgasmic meditation session by first setting up a "nest." They place a blanket on the floor for the woman to lie down on and a number of pillows to support her legs and head. The woman then takes off her pants and underwear, reclines, and opens her legs. Her partner sits down on a cushion to her right, remaining fully clothed. He puts his left leg over her body and his right leg under hers. Then he sets a timer for fifteen minutes, puts on a pair of latex gloves, and puts lubrication on one finger. He looks down and poetically describes the woman's vulva to her. He asks for permission to touch her. When she grants it, he puts his thumb into her introitus with his right hand. With his left he gently begins stroking the upper left-hand quadrant of her clitoris, applying only very gentle pressure. This continues for the remainder of the allotted time, sometimes wordlessly, some-times with the woman offering guidance or her partner sharing observations or physical feelings. When the timer ends (usually heralded by the "Bell" setting on an iPhone), the man cups his hand over the woman's vulva, providing firm pressure to "ground" her. Then the session ends. He covers her with a towel, and the two share what the OM-ers call "frames." The man might say, as one did in an instructional video I watched: "I felt a bright, thin gold pulse from the tip of my finger up to my chest." The woman might respond, as she did in the same video: "There was a mo-ment where you slowed the stroke and stopped for a split second and I felt a deep electrical exhale move through the upper part of my body." Following these statements the OM is complete. The woman puts her clothes back on, the nest is put away, and the two get on with their day.

After this meeting I went back to my apartment and watched more of the organization's videos on the Internet. They mostly showed couples. There sat Marcus, sitting with his partner, a woman named Hadassah. In reality-television-style testimonials they said things like "Once I started to OM I realized how much was available," and "OM-ing helped me find my voice. It's not just the secret to better relationships, it's the secret to a better life," and "You are sitting on a volcano and you don't know it," and

"The turn-on is there the whole time." Marcus and Hadassah looked at each other with love.

I went back to Moss Street the next day. The founder of One-Taste, Nicole Daedone, was lecturing that evening, in what Alisha had said was her first public appearance in months. Daedone had been working on her next book, about the "OneTaste theory of relationships." The lecture was to be webcast via her Facebook page and both the live audience and the Web audience would have the opportunity to ask questions.

Walking over to the OneTaste facility through the bleak streets of SOMA I was conscious of weariness settling over me. I was interested in their project but I did not want to have to talk to these people again. They demanded an enthusiasm and a positivity it exhausted me to have to muster and present. As I approached the location, I saw the sickly depressed man walking with a female companion across the street. He still wore his curious draped outfit of white, including what appeared to be linen white culottes, which exposed his stockinged ankles and Birkenstock sandals. One ankle appeared to be supported by a tan ACE bandage, but I had merely conditioned myself, because of his white attire, to think of him as a sort of hospital patient, oppressed with an unknown malady. In reality he was simply wearing a single brown sock on his left foot. I hung back to avoid overtaking them and having to acknowledge that we had both attended the group meeting last night, shared "intimacies," and would therefore have to introduce ourselves to each other. In my efforts to avoid this encounter, I took a wrong turn and arrived by way of a circuitous route, walking back toward OneTaste after having overshot my destination by several blocks.

Ahead of me, a woman in a long mustard-yellow skirt

scanned the numbers of the buildings on Moss Street. She opened the door of OneTaste and disappeared inside. I followed her, passing through the velvet curtains into the entryway, which was now filled with people. The clipboard phalanx remembered my name and welcomed me back as if I were an old friend. I greeted Justine Dawson, who did public relations for the organization. In the room where we had sat yesterday, the seats had been rearranged into rows. Lights, cameras, and cords gave the space the appearance of a floodlit production studio and added an air of significance to the moment. These arrangements all oriented themselves toward a simple tableau: two high stools and an end table with a white calla lily and two glasses on it. Two bottles of Perrier stood beneath the table unopened.

Nicole Daedone was immediately recognizable, not simply from her photos online but because of the acolytes who now flocked excitedly around her. More than this I knew her by her charisma, which had a physical component. She was in her mid-forties and tall. She wore a delicate bias-cut shift of milky white that revealed her décolletage. Her hair was dyed a pale gold and she wore gold hoop earrings. She was tan and her long legs were bare and impeccably depilated. She wore a pair of black suede wedge heels and a ring that was a sort of half gyroscope of diamonds. As the audience waited for her speech, their attention was drawn to her, half-monitoring what she would do and what she might say as they carried out their own conversations.

The organizers turned off the music. Daedone came down the side of the aisle on the right and sat in front of the audience on one of the stools. After a brief introduction, where she was introduced as the "originator of the practice of orgasmic meditation," Daedone was left alone on stage. She began with the deliberate gesture the moderators had used the previous night: the calm, wise, glance around the room, until the audience became aware of a change and fell silent. Then Daedone began speaking, in a quiet, conversational tone.

She teaches, she said, one thing: "I teach about desire and the fulfillment of desire." Women have been trained, she continued, to think that men don't want them to be happy. But desire was not about indulgence. It was not Harlequin romances or bonbons or shopping. It was the antithesis of that, an "unbelievably stringent mistress," and the best way Daedone had discovered to feel desire was the experience called orgasmic meditation, a thing for which there was no "cultural context."

"How many people know what orgasmic meditation is?" she asked. Many people in the room, which held at least one hundred people, raised their hands. Daedone nodded. "We've actually gotten to the point where we sound like we make sense."

Daedone then proceeded to tell her story, the details of which were filled in with each retelling I heard over the course of several weeks. She grew up in Los Gatos, California, with her single mother, in what she frequently alluded to as a boisterous and emotional family of Sicilian descent. She had sex for the first time when she was sixteen, got pregnant, then had an abortion. She attended San Francisco State University, and in her twenties began to collaborate with a friend on an art gallery. She described herself then as an uptight and controlling person, who dressed in tight black dresses with white pearls, who ate well and practiced yoga and surpassed all contemporary indices of personal fortitude and accomplishment. She had boyfriends, but there was no indication, in her early twenties, that she would go on to devote her life to spreading gospels of sexuality. She did not feel capable of sharing joy with other people. "I was a bitch," she said.

Then, when she was twenty-seven, Daedone received a phone call and learned that her father was on the verge of death. Daedone only rarely mentions her father in lectures, and doesn't explain where he fit in her portrait of her expressive Sicilian family. Daedone's father died in prison, convicted of child molestation. She has said that he did not harm her as a child, but that she had spent many years of her life "choosing the option of the powerful-victim identity."

She told the story of his death in mystical terms: she ascended in the hospital elevator toward his deathbed, and suddenly experienced a singular feeling, not of sadness but of rapture. Time seemed to dilate. The air in the elevator took on an aquatic quality. For a moment, every other aspect of her life faded. When the elevator doors opened, Daedone had lost the illusion of purpose. In the days that followed her father's death her resolve collapsed. A breakdown followed, until, in another epiphanic moment, while running through Yerba Buena Gardens a few days later, Daedone heard a voice, clear as a bell. It said, "You will not leave any part of yourself behind."

I knew what she meant. Losing oneself, in the local context, was a reasonable fear. Strange lives are led in Northern California, where one intellectual stumble can turn you into a wild-eyed apostle of pet acupuncture or shadow healing. It is the national headquarters of bronzed mystics speaking into wireless microphones, promising all the keys to "unlocking your potential." An army of them waited, in thousands of YouTube videos, to validate pain and propose solutions. In mentioning her own skepticism about the magic formulas Daedone was really addressing my own skepticism, and that of the other people in the room, who might see her speech as just another sales pitch.

Until the death of her father, Daedone had dabbled in spirituality, but now she waded into an active exploration of New Age ideologies of self-help, self-improvement, and self-navigation. She began her training at a panspiritual "mystery school," taking a vow of silence there for the better part of a year. She deepened her exploration into Taoism and Zen, part of what she later would see as an attempt to reject the messy business of death, sex, and the body. In speeches she refers to mysterious mentors, including three women who absorbed her into a coven and a "thug guru" who meted out harsh truths. She speaks of having once lived in an "acid house" and of other experiments living communally. She practiced meditation, vegetarianism, and, for two and a half years, celibacy. She concluded her initial three-year foray into the esoteric with a plan to pursue a life of celibacy and monasticism at the San Francisco Zen Center. Before this renunciation, however, she went to a party.

At the party Daedone met a Buddhist, an older man in his seventies. They began discussing sex. He invited her to try "a practice." He explained that for the practice she would lie down, she would disrobe from the waist down, and he would stroke her clitoris for fifteen minutes. "I'll stroke you," he said. "You don't have to stroke me back."

Daedone told this story to a deeply attentive audience, who was so eager to laugh that they would find hilarity in the mildest of verbal miscues or the blandest of risqué jokes. When she would use a colloquialism, or when she would mime a toke from a joint, the room would explode with laughter. Her speech did not follow any easily summarized rhetorical structure; thoughts began, but they did not always conclude, or would be rendered diffuse after drifting through non sequiturs. Chronologies were hazy. She made statements that had protean referents, like the idea of "becoming the person you were always meant to be" or "accessing your inner teacher." Still, the failures of chronology or logic did not affect her power over the room, because her strength as an orator lay in the intensely personal nature of her disclosures, the ease of her gestures, and her glossy appearance.

Her session with the man from the party, she said, indicated to her that "something more was possible." She had established a sexual connection with a person without having had sex with him. She had not had to worry about whether he was attracted to her, whether he was honest, if he would call the next day, who would pay for dinner. The "deliberate orgasm," as the practice was called, was neither sex nor masturbation. It unlinked sexual experience from love and romance in the way that casual sex never had for her.

"Rather than actually feeling the sex I would feel the relationship," Daedone said of her life before OM. "I was very sneaky about never confronting my genitals as genitals."

She meant, I think, that the stroking practice was a sexual technique that allowed for an intimate connection but preserved an emotional distance, a sexual practice that allowed one to be close to another person while remaining autonomous. Her partner needed only to know what he was doing and respect the boundaries of the process. She did not have to love or even like him. I saw the appeal: if this strange method of sexual communication between friends could be available to everyone, then a feeling of sexual connection need not be such a rare thing, but as common as friendship itself. It could happen abundantly, with people who failed every ideal of perfection.

Daedone now focused her research on orgasm, a term she used not according to its dictionary definition as a moment of climax but rather to refer to a generalized idea of sexual energy in the world. What she began to hypothesize was that love and relationships in an era of sexual freedom followed an obsolete system of "crossed wires." She described it as a difference between the map and the territory. Men and women believed that certain sexual behaviors would reward them with certain results: fidelity would be recognized with long and happy marriages, or honesty would be met with honesty. When these ideas of sexual propriety failed to deliver the expected results, people mistakenly blamed personal deficiencies rather than systemic ones.

As many have before her, Daedone suspected the problem lay not in people, but in the network of rules and expectations that govern adult life. In particular, the tendency of women to link sexual desire with so many arbitrary expectations and consequences that they cannot focus on the sexual experience itself. Orgasmic meditation, she concluded, would be the neutral space in which focus on the body could happen without the interference of romantic stories or behavioral conditioning.

She did not realize all of this right away, but only after years of research. In 2000, by then in her thirties, she met Rob Kandell, who later became chief operating officer of OneTaste. Kandell had undertaken a similar navigation through California self-help, doing Landmark Forum workshops and studying the literature published by More University, an intentional community started in 1968 that produced reports on its "lifestyle experiments." He told me, vaguely, that he met Daedone at "a social mixer with people engaged in sexuality." Kandell was married at the time, but he, his wife, and Daedone started going to sexuality workshops together. Soon they started discussing a curriculum for their own workshops.

Justine Dawson, OneTaste's public relations woman, called it the search for a "clean, well-lit place, for people to talk about this stuff." In relation to a New Age organization with evident roots in the human potential movement of the 1960s, the aphorism was meant to dispel the lingering fear of fanatics and cults, of the aprons and lentil soups of the old male-dominated New Communalism. As Dawson explained to me: "There were other people teaching in communities but it often felt like there wasn't necessarily the most urban, open, clean, clear feeling about it . . . it was sidelined as hippie or backwoods." When she started her study,

most of the people teaching deliberate orgasm were men; Daedone wanted to create something woman-centric, a technique
that was carried by women but that did not exclude men from
the process.

In 2004, Kandell sold his house in the Outer Richmond area
and invested the money in a new organization, now called the
OneTaste Urban Retreat Center. Daedone signed a lease on a
warehouse at 1074 Folsom Street, in which an initial group of
twelve people would live communally. They opened their doors
on July 30, 2004, with the tag line "A Pleasurable Place for Your
Body to Be." Their stated mission was "to bring orgasm back into
the world conversation and back into our bodies." The warehouse had a space that could be rented for private events. It had
a store. They offered yoga and meditation classes, workshops,
massages, and books about sexuality. A 2005 article in the *San
Francisco Chronicle* described their naked yoga classes as "trans-
forming, not titillating."

The residents of the warehouse also experimented among
themselves. Daedone does not speak in great detail about this,
other than calling it the phase of "research and development." The
rooms in the warehouse had no doors. At its most active, fifty
people lived communally in the space, essentially volunteer
human research subjects inhabiting a petri dish. They would rise
each morning early, at 7:00 a.m., and OM. Then they would
undergo a group session called Withholds, a discussion technique
that Daedone had learned from Victor Baranco, the founder of
More University, where communal residents voiced suppressed
thoughts or feelings about one another. Then they wrote in jour-
nals or practiced yoga.

The sexual research of the house's residents went beyond the
practice of orgasmic meditation, although residents would OM
two or three times a day. A person with whom one shared a bed

was called a "research partner," and research partners would invite each other over for "sleepovers." Through sex and discussion about sex they pushed the boundaries of jealousy: an awareness of being near a partner, for example, while he slept with someone new, or forcing people to continue to communicate with each other even in the middle of the worst emotional upheavals. They explored the particularities of sexual responses by women who had experienced trauma or had eating disorders. They looked at how a woman's sexual experience might evolve with age. They discussed how a man should respond when a woman starts crying during sex, or how a man can discern a woman's sexual satisfaction if she does not vocalize her enjoyment. The communal nature of the experience was essential. If a difficulty arose, the resident would have the rest of the group there to discuss the problem. If the world at large condemned their sexuality, the numbers of the group would reinforce the worth of the experimentation.

According to one former resident, who spent three or four months in the warehouse in 2008 when he was in his mid-twenties, "there wasn't that much sex happening," despite "the sounds of orgasm rippling through the warehouse through the day" as people OM-ed with each other. As a man, he was not allowed to be stroked unless the woman offered in return. ("We teach men not to ask and women not to offer for at least a year, or six months," said Kandell, of the "male stroking practice," which does in fact exist but the specifics of which are obscured to all but the more committed members of OneTaste. The idea is to eliminate the notion of sex as a reciprocal servicing contract, and to encourage women who consider the needs of others before their own to learn how to receive rather than give.) The former warehouse resident found his experience living there beneficial, especially the work to eradicate gender-based preconceptions about sexuality. He felt he had genuinely learned to perceive and read what the OM-ers call "turn-on," or the body's physical responses to the presence of another person. He gave me a summary of their theories about privileging the drives of the body, or "limbic system," over the reasoning of the mind, or "cortex." The downside of living in the warehouse was the heavy focus on recruitment, the pressure to make OneTaste a proselytizing endeavor.

"They were, to my chagrin, very much motivated to bring people in by selling the program," he said. OneTaste earned revenue by charging for workshops and coaching, and anyone who traded their e-mail address or phone number in exchange for the right to watch a video or attend a lecture could expect a long series of solicitations. The first workshop he took was very beneficial to him; the second class was "bullshit." He found the teaching strangely anti-love, or at least averse to the building up of intimacy between two people at the expense of others, elevating instead an idea of wider-ranging connectedness. The warehouse was not welcoming to those who fell in love. "I very much enjoy intimacy," he said, and ultimately concluded the OneTaste way was not for him. It took him time to reintegrate back into the world of mainstream expectations, to remember how love and sex worked without the structure of OM-ing.

Daedone emerged from this "research and development phase" having refined and codified the system and practice of orgasmic meditation, which she says provides a stable foundation from which to experiment. OM-ing every day, she said, gave her more security from which to pursue more emotionally demanding situations. (When I met her she was attempting a year of "extreme non-monogamy.") At the end of 2008, OneTaste abandoned its warehouse and moved its offices and residence to a former single-room-occupancy hotel nearby, which had the advantage of having doors. They brought their numbers down to twelve residents. "The heat in the warehouse, I think, was too high for the public," said Kandell.

By the time OneTaste was profiled for the first time in *The New York Times* in 2009, the organization had adopted a tone of friendly ambiguity. The opacity about what happened at One-Taste beyond the orgasmic meditation it publicly advertised allowed the organization to appeal to both monogamous couples and women who thought of themselves as reluctant sexual explorers. Daedone's great hope was that one day asking someone for an OM would be like "inviting someone for a cup of tea."

That night, before her live audience, she described how the practice works. She set up the "nest" of pillows and one of her colleagues volunteered (remaining fully clothed, in this instance). Nicole set her subject in position, then put her hand on her legs. "I'll feel the difference between the sensation in her body, and the sensation in mine," she explained. Then she would put lubrication on her fingers, set a timer for fifteen minutes, and begin stroking. "So if her clitoris were a clock" (the room found this hilarious), "it would be the one o'clock position. And you're just going to stroke there, up, down, up, down, up, down, up down." The lecture ended in wild applause.

In order to try an orgasmic meditation, the first step was attending a one-day workshop at OneTaste to get "certified" to OM. The workshop cost $97. Justine told me I was lucky, because I would have the rare treat of viewing a live demonstration, and Nicole would be there in the morning.

After signing a release that said, among other things, that we understood that "OM-ing is not psychotherapy," the workshop began with the same round of games as before, although this time discussion was led by Nicole. She looked casually sexy in a short gray dress that revealed her long legs and bare arms and tan suede high-heeled boots. Again, in response to the question about the motives that brought us to the workshop, I responded, "Curious."

Nicole challenged me. "You say that but I'm sensing some irritation." I was irritated. The man to my left reeked of booze, was red-faced and bright-eyed, and I was pretty sure that whatever was in his coffee cup, at ten in the morning, was not coffee. He would laugh loudly and frequently and would turn and stare at my profile. He radiated a grasping need. I felt he had come to the room with a question and had singled me out as an answer to that question. As long as I was conscious of his presence I felt almost nauseated with anxiety. The room was warm and oppressive, and the fifty people in the semicircle formed a tight wall. I could not take notes without attracting attention, but needed to take notes. I could have said all this but instead I pretended I was relaxed and enjoying myself, even though I felt only more anxiety for having been singled out by Nicole.

She questioned other people, too, and could come down harshly. Winning her approval or earning her notice became a part of the room's dynamic. A man sitting on the floor confessed himself a skeptic of the benefits of orgasmic meditation, and Nicole bristled. "Then why are you here?" she asked. "I'm not here to convince you." A medical resident at Stanford University, a divorcee still in her twenties with whom I had been chatting earlier, said, "I'm here because I haven't had an orgasm in five years." When another woman introduced herself, Nicole interrupted her with an air of psychic prognosis. "Are you from San Diego?" she asked. "I'm from the Bay Area," replied the woman. Nicole stared at her intently. Then she looked around the room.

"What's the 'It's Hard Out Here for a Pimp' movie?" she asked. "*Hustle and Flow*," someone yelled out. Nicole nodded and looked back at the woman. "It's hard to be a witch when everyone around you is normal," she said.

We broke for lunch. I went to a nearby café followed, to my dismay, by the man who had been sitting next to me, who ordered a beer. Several other people joined us. One of them, a woman in her early twenties named Lauren, was enthusiastically raising funds to try to enter OneTaste's coaching program, which cost $13,000.

Lunch was a relief from the frenetic atmosphere of a room where everyone was talking about sex. I waited until my neighbor sat down with his beer then chose a seat on the other side of the room. When we arrived back at the workshop, we were all much calmer. Alisha and Rob led a discussion about the morning's events. Suddenly Nicole stood up from her seat in the back row and came to the front. She had changed costume, and was now wearing jeans and a draping, oatmeal-colored cowl-neck sweater. She was worried, she said, that the energy had gone out of the room. She lamented that we had all returned to our usual, comfortable state of sexual repression. This was true. I felt much more relaxed. Nicole said this was a mistake. "A group of people gets very uncomfortable when things get hot," she said. "This practice is *necessarily* uncomfortable." So before we proceeded, she asked us to go around the room and talk about our feelings some more. "The whole thing is for each person in this room to become who they are," she announced. "The soul isn't just connected to the heart, it's connected to cocks and pussies."

We continued going around the room, sharing our feelings, Nicole periodically stopping to interrogate people further. A young olive-skinned man said that he loved women but felt like a different person when he was having sex. She stopped him.

"Are you Italian?" she asked. He was, he said. She looked at him thoughtfully.

"Women love to fuck," she told him. "They have no desire deeper than to devour you." I had started taking notes again, but at this I stopped. Her eyes now scanned the room and rested on me. "What?" she asked. "You look skeptical."

I admitted that as interested as I was in being in a room with so much openly expressed desire, I was feeling hemmed in by it. I said I guessed I liked to have more control about who I could be sexual with, and that unwanted advances made me anxious. As much as I might "love to fuck," it was usually only true for one guy out of several hundred, and sexual interest from the rest bothered me.

In response to this, Nicole told a story about a guy who was leaving lascivious comments on her website. Every day, the man wrote to her how much he wanted to fuck her, about all the nasty things that he would do to her. She ignored him for a while, but then finally confronted him, asked him for his number, texted him, and said, "Okay, let's do this. Come on over."

Nothing. He did not respond. She had proven herself bigger than his desire. By inviting rather than repelling this man, she had put herself in a position of power over him. Women, she explained, tend to receive sexual desire with anxiety. When Nicole walks into a room and perceives someone's sexual interest directed her way, she now internally acknowledges it instead of pretending to be unaware of it or doing everything possible to diminish it. She monitors the response of her body, specifically her genitals, to the other people in the room. She will even talk about this in speeches: "At all times there isn't a moment when I'm awake that my ambient attention isn't anchored to my genitals," she said in a video I later watched online. "I can tell you at any moment—not that you're going to ask—what's happening in my genitals.

Right now my genitals are slightly swollen, they're switched out a little bit, it feels like there's a light layer, almost of like sweat or perspiration, it feels really warm and there's a buzzing around my introitus. At any moment I keep my attention there, and if you keep your attention there you stay grounded with what's happening. If you can keep your attention located on the most intense domain of the body, then nothing out here matters." Now, as a mental exercise, she makes a point of identifying who in the room she "wants to fuck."

This statement offended my propriety. Shouldn't I have the right to be in the world without having to contend with male desire? My whole life I had received strangers attempting to flirt with me with the graciousness of a fence post. It had always filled me with annoyance. I could never take it lightly, as I saw my friends could, when we were interrupted at a bar in the middle of an interesting conversation to endure a dull performance by a man. My first impulse was always to indicate that I wanted to be left alone as quickly as possible. Of all the things Nicole Daedone said to me, however, the idea of acknowledging and accepting the sexuality in a room, feeling it, naming it, and inhabiting it, was a kernel of a thing that I kept trying to dismiss but found I was unable to stop thinking about. To walk into a room and concentrate on the way my body responded to the people in it was a sexual inquiry I could conduct privately, without any risk. After thinking of what Nicole had said, I discerned a duplicity at work in the archive of my own perceptions, whereby I had carefully excised my sexual awareness of other people from the naming of my experiences and pretended my own physical responses had not happened. I wondered what this façade of asexuality had cost me in confidence and decisiveness. Had I made choices on false pretenses? To shift my perception meant only that I began letting myself name when I wanted to stare at someone, or that I fought the impulse to look away when someone stared at me. I tried to notice the catalog of subtle urges or repulsions that I would never name or discuss out loud. I experimented with my responses to getting hit on or hollered at on the street, forcing myself to chat or nod, letting myself experience the unsettled feeling that came with a sexual overture, just sitting in the feeling and trying to know it, instead of immediately trying to close it down. It became apparent how much energy I expended in being affronted, or wondering whether I should be affronted. Other women at OneTaste would talk about conducting similar personal experiments. They might mention that they had spent a week sitting with their legs spread in public, so as to test out the sense of entitlement or ownership over a space.

The time now came for Nicole to give a demo of the practice of orgasmic meditation. We took a short break and the staff set up a massage table covered in pillows. Justine Dawson took off her jeans, and the look that passed between Nicole and Justine was one of complete trust and mutual assurance. They were friends who knew each other well. Sitting up while Nicole explained her process, Justine looked unembarrassed and cheerful. She was a fair-haired woman in her mid-thirties, slim and small. Once Nicole had adjusted the pillows, Justine lay back and splayed her legs.

"The first thing I'm going to do is safeport her," said Nicole. She told Justine that her hands were cold. Then she described Justine's vulva to the room. This was where Daedone could be her most poetic, evoking seashells and flower petals. As house style, OneTaste always used the terms *pussy* and *cock*. When I asked someone why, the response was that the problem with female genitalia was that it was difficult to describe the whole thing—the word *vagina*, commonly used, at least in the medical sense of the word, refers only to one part of things. So, too, *clitoris*, *vulva, introitus, labia,* and all the other parts. Nicole, former student of semantics, had therefore decided to use *pussy.* "I'm super big on reclamation of terms," she told me.

She put lube on her fingers. She explained that she and Justine were old friends who got regularly tested for sexually transmitted infections. We should always use latex gloves. "Sex is not worth dying for," she said. She explained that she would be touching Justine's clitoris with no more pressure than rubbing a finger across an eyelid. Around the room, men and women touched the pads of their fingertips to their eyelids. Then she began her performance.

It was like watching a medium in a séance, or an evangelical taken by a spirit. Nicole's face assumed a look of intense concentration. She had her right arm draped over Justine's leg, and used her left arm to stroke. Justine almost immediately started moaning. As she stroked, Daedone would throw her head down and then toss her hair back again, biting her lip and gazing heavenward as she tried new configurations. Beneath her arms Justine quaked and shivered. The room was silent and rapt. The man to my right began to inhale and exhale with deep, meditative breaths. The face of the man on my other side took on a deeper red flush. Justine never reached a recognizable climax. There was no clear peak followed by a lull. Her left arm grasped feebly at the air. Her legs vibrated. During the performance, Nicole asked several women up to the massage table, where they put their hands on Justine's leg and felt the currents of feeling washing over her. Justine's vocalizations were consistently loud but varied in tone. When the timer sounded, Nicole ended the practice with a firm downward stroke. She closed Justine's labia. She took a clean towel, placed her hand over it, and pulled it downward through her hand. Then she covered Justine with the towel. Justine lay motionless.

Following this, we had a lecture from a doctor from Berkeley about the benefits of regularly flooding the female body with oxytocin through orgasms. Then Daedone left and Alisha and Rob returned to their duties. Now we stacked the chairs and faced each other in two lines, men on one side and women on the other. This set of exercises involved an escalating series of interrogations followed by touching. With each exercise, we would step to our right, so as to be in contact with a different person. The man would be asked to describe the face of the woman in front of him, and vice versa, with instructions to include mention of all the lines, blemishes, or errors in makeup. As a man described to me the traces of my makeup, a blemish on my chin, and other flaws in my appearance that I had convinced myself were too small to be noticeable, I felt a unique experience of horror. We stood in front of each other and repeatedly asked the question "What do you desire?"—a question to which I could only stammer meager responses. I was conscious for the first time of the flat white screen that rolled down when I considered such a question, the opaque shadows of movement behind it. A vacant search bar waited, cursor blinking, for ideas that I, who did not consider an idea an idea until it was expressed in language, had never expressed in language. What I said I desired was to surrender to another person without having to explain what I wanted.

The men took the wrists of the women and gently stroked them with their fingers in an up-down motion. We stroked each other's shoulders and then interviewed each other about what we had felt. After it was over, I did not take up the option to partner with someone else from the workshop and try an orgasmic meditation for the first time. I felt physically exhausted and emotionally drained. Every time I thought of the older man whose shoulders I had petted I felt a deep repulsion. There is a reason for boundaries, I told myself, not at all certain if it was true but knowing that I was certainly more comfortable with boundaries.

I avoided all eye contact with people looking for partners, and quickly walked to the Muni stop and caught the bus home, where I bought takeout Vietnamese food, an ice cream sandwich, and a bottle of wine and watched the Norman conquest episode of Simon Schama's *History of Britain*, my last birthday present from the ex-boyfriend whose average response time to my e-mails was now four to six weeks, if he responded at all.

A few days later I was sitting in the Harvey Milk branch of the San Francisco Public Library when Justine Dawson called me. I felt a twinge of panic and ignored the call, then forced myself out into the sunshine, where a cold wind was blowing, to return it. Justine asked how the class had been. I told her that it had been overwhelming for me. She again suggested I try the practice. She said that she could not tell me who to OM with or set it up for me, but that if I joined the secret orgasmic meditation group on Facebook I could message a couple of men who might be interested. I joined the Facebook group, and soon received a friendly message from Eli, the man who had led the first meeting I had attended. I liked that he did orgasmic meditation all the time, so that it would be uneventful for him. I asked him to OM, he said yes, and we arranged for a Thursday at noon session at OneTaste. It was a sunny day, and I went running that morning, then showered carefully and shaved my legs. I walked to 47 Moss Street slowly, not listening to music through headphones. I passed a man carrying a bongo drum and a tambourine, a paper sign in a window that said "The Center for Sex and Culture Has Moved," and a lunatic woman with her pants down around her knees, performing a fanciful ballet dance.

The building on Moss Street was still and quiet. I went through the heavy velvet curtains that divided the room and closed off the event space from the entryway. Two affiliates of OneTaste were there. One, whose name was Henry, gave me a pint glass filled with green tea and I sat on the couch. Eli entered with Matthew, an older man whom I had met the night of Nicole's first lecture. Eli and I went upstairs. Off the landing were three carpeted rooms furnished with pillows and chairs. Eli went to gather supplies from a closet: one pillow for him to sit on, a smaller pillow for my head, a woolen yoga blanket, yoga mat, and towels for me to lie on. "Is there anything I can do to make you feel more secure?" he asked. I said I didn't think so. His presence, above all the ease and casualness with which he did these things, was reassuring enough.

The room was small, its walls painted gray. It had two yellow chairs, white curtains, and exposed wood-beamed ceilings. It was very warm in the room and Eli opened a window to let in a breeze. We made small talk. I learned that he was twenty-eight years old and had quit his job at Apple to work for OneTaste. He asked me which direction I wanted to face, and then, perhaps sensing my inability to decide, said, "Or I can just decide." I chose to have my head toward the window, feet toward the door. He announced each step he was going to take methodically. He was going to take off his shoes. Then he said, "Now it's the time when you take off your pants." This was the moment, in a gynecological exam or a bikini wax, when the practitioner left the room, but Eli stayed, and I took off my pants. I asked if I should take off my socks. "Your choice," he said. I took off my socks. "I'll take mine off, too," he said.

He guided me into a sitting position and took my leg over his arm. I felt very secure. I could feel his leg against my leg; his arm supported my arm. He set the timer on his phone. He took several deep breaths and began massaging my legs. The pressure of his hands on my legs felt nice. He put on latex gloves. "Now I'm going to begin stroking," he said.

Before he had begun, I had thought I was feeling aroused. I could feel the breeze from the window over me. I thought of Justine's boisterous display and I worried I might reveal something of myself I didn't want to reveal to a stranger. Once he began touching me, however, I performed, and experienced, detachment. I didn't have anything that resembled climax or an orgasm, or feel stimulation in the way that I would have with a vibrator. I felt no desire to have sex with the man holding my legs, but feeling his breath rise and fall against my leg brought a feeling of deep, intense comfort. I was not transported by rapture. This was quiet and still. I concentrated on breathing and feeling the pressure of his body. At one point he said, thoughtfully, "I feel a deep swelling at the base of my cock." Then the bell on his iPhone chimed and it was over. We shared "frames." I had trouble thinking of anything to say and remember only that whatever it was I said felt somewhat fictional. Then I put on my clothes and left. I did this two more times, both with Eli. I never reached the point of eagerness. I turned down several other invitations and canceled on people with whom I had scheduled appointments. The third time I tried orgasmic meditation was in a room with other people also practicing. I climaxed, or "went over," as the OneTaste people put it, as I stared at a coffee urn on a table. I felt sad afterward, as I did sometimes after sex. It had not been so different from sex, where some orgasms happened because I concentrated and willed them. A climax could be perfunctory. It could be just another form of service to another person, to give him a sense of satisfaction. I could climax even during sex I did not enjoy.

For months I pretended that what I saw at OneTaste was so far beyond the boundaries of my day-to-day reality that it didn't affect me. This was easy to do because what the people at OneTaste did was very strange. At the time, I would have rather socialized with any other group of people than them. I disliked them. I preferred the company of people who did not insist on sympathetic eye contact, who did not need to talk about all of their feelings at every instance, who drank and smoked cigarettes. I felt more comfortable in situations where I had the right to remain maladjusted, to leave some feelings undisclosed, to acknowledge and enjoy the prospect of my own mortality. Their language made me cringe. They would describe themselves as feeling "tumesced" and used the word *penetrate* to indicate a personal breakthrough. They liked to use *sex* as a verb instead of a noun: "My sexing changed," said Rob Kandell. "So how I OM informed how I sex, and how I sex started to inform my OM-ing."

I would see people I had met through OneTaste on the street in the Mission, or run into them at the Rainbow Food Co-op, the great temple of antioxidant and raw snack foods. Once one asked me out, inviting me to a tea lounge on Fourteenth Street that many of them frequented. He wore a beaded necklace, and he stared into my eyes. "It's an open space," he said of the tea lounge. "It doesn't have the darkness or oppression of a bar."

"I like bars," I replied snottily.

After I left San Francisco that summer, OneTaste kept calling. First it was the occasional text message from Marcus or Eli or Henry asking if I wanted to OM, to which I would happily reply that I was no longer in San Francisco. Then members of the organization would occasionally call to invite me to a lecture or a workshop.

The updates of the meditators filled my Facebook newsfeed

with their daily epiphanies. I continued to read them and would watch their video testimonies.

"The moment you realize you've built a life based on 'stroke for your own pleasure,'" one would write.

"The (much earlier) moment when you realize that you haven't. And that you could," another would reply.

"Thank you," the original poster would write. "And the much later moment when you realize there is no going back. And that you couldn't."

"So, so good!" someone else wrote.

But if their followers, or those of the Esalen Institute ("pioneering deep change in self and society") or the Landmark Forum ("create a future of your own design") or the Zen Center ("may all beings realize their true nature") or Lafayette Morehouse ("you are perfect, the world is perfect, and you are totally responsible for your life") or the Pathways Institute ("the exploration of human consciousness leading to your personal, professional and spiritual wisdom, skills and fulfillment"), seemed self-obsessed, it was because so many doctrines—marriage, the nuclear family, sexual taboos, diet, gender—had successfully been exploded. The privilege of being middle class in America in the twenty-first century meant that most of the pressing questions in life were left to choice. Who should I have sex with when I'm single? What should I eat for dinner? What should I do to earn money? There was limited ancient guidance on such historically preposterous questions. The difficulty of actually choosing which rules to live by invited extensive self-examination.

There was an idea that greater gender equality had not brought equal sexual fulfillment, and most commonly held ideas about sex were still oriented toward masculine ideas about orgasm and desire. People felt sexually "liberated"—they were trying a wider range of things on a broader scale than perhaps at any other time in American history, and although sexual repression lingered, the problem was often not sexual repression. It was that the women who saw promise in pursuing sexual openness often found themselves battling their own feelings: trying to control attachment, pretending to enjoy something that hurt or annoyed them, defining sexiness by images they had seen rather than knowing what they wanted. The people at OneTaste were looking for a method to arrive at a more authentic and stable experience of sexual openness, one that came from immanent desire instead of an anxiety to please. Their method was strange, but at least they believed in the possibility.

INTERNET PORN

The first legal images of penetration were published in the magazine *Private* in 1965. And to think of everything that has happened since then ... What was called porn, by the second decade of the twenty-first century, was a paring down of plot, performance, and romance to the very basics of efficient sexual stimulation. The ten-minute video clips, organized into a grid on websites and indexed by interest, were, in relation to the history of porn, like the pinnacle of a mountainous landfill. Seagulls circled above and bulldozers aerated below, unearthing martini glasses, smoking jackets, Leather Goddesses of Phobos, alt.breast .net. Yesterday, without putting in any credit card information, you watched three tanned hard bodies winch a woman up against a gently swaying palm tree and today you watched a butch woman with very hairy legs and one pierced nipple face-fuck another woman with a strap-on and tomorrow you will watch what the computer says is a cum-craving hottie feeling a ripping hard cock banging her pleasure hole. Or you didn't watch it at all. The culture had an abstract idea, "porn," which for some people meant particular websites, search terms, and somatic memories but for others was only a vague menace that flickered obscurely in the dark.

Porn caused my friends a lot of anxiety. Some people enjoyed watching it as part of a daily routine. Some felt enslaved by their desire for it. Others saw their real-world sexual experiences reduced to a corny mimicry of porn, and wished they could somehow return to a time when porn was less ubiquitous, or was just soft-focus tan people having unadventurous sex by a swimming pool. Since more men watched porn than women, the occasional imbalance of knowledge caused distress all around and was perceived at times as an imbalance of power. Porn made people jealous, it hurt feelings, it made them worry about whether their partners were attracted to them or to the kind of people they watched in porn, who might have a different hair color, skin color, or bra size. Because porn loves the taboo, it could also be racist and misogynist.

It was tempting, now, to think that sex before Internet porn had been less complicated. There were sexual acts in porn that it would not occur to many people to attempt. We had more expectations about what kind of sex to have, and how many people should be involved, and what to say, and what our bodies should look like, than we might have had at a time when sexual imagery was less available to us.

People who liked porn described their desire to watch it as similar to wanting to watch videos of cats climbing into boxes in the middle of doing one's taxes. Alternatively, it was like going to a café alone and eating a piece of cake in the middle of the afternoon. It gave temporary fulfillment to a need. It primed them for masturbation, which they might do to relax, procrastinate, or fall asleep. But porn united all of the possibilities, including the ones we didn't want to have.

Public Disgrace was an online pornography series that advertised itself as "women bound, stripped, and punished in public." It was the creation of a San Francisco–based porn director and dominatrix named Princess Donna Dolore. Princess Donna conceived of the project in 2008, during her fourth year of working for the pornography company Kink.com. In addition to directing, Donna performed in the shoots, though she was not usually the lead.

When Princess Donna scouted locations for Public Disgrace she looked for small windows (they needed to be blacked out) and spaces (they needed to look crowded). For outdoor shoots she usually worked in Europe, where public obscenity laws are more forgiving. Before each shoot, Princess Donna coordinated with the female lead to establish what she liked or didn't like and produced a checklist of what the performer would take from her civilian audience. Some models accepted only groping, some had rules against slapping, and some were willing to be fingered or spat on by the audience.

Princess Donna had experience as an orchestrator of complicated fantasies of group sex, public sex, and violent sex. Such situations tended to be, as she put it, "kind of tricky to live out in real life." Her role, as a director and performer, was to both initiate and contain the extremity. She was also a deft manipulator of the human body. Female performers trusted her to extend the boundaries of their physical capacities.

The job description for Public Disgrace, posted at Kink.com, read: "Sex between male dominant and female submissive; domination by female and male dom; secure bondage, gags, hoods, fondling, flogging, and forced orgasms with vibrators." For four to five hours of work, performers earned between $1,100 and $1,300, plus bonuses for extra sex acts with cameo performers who could show a clean bill of health.

A few weeks after I arrived in San Francisco, I attended a Public Disgrace shoot. The shoots were open to the public, a public that was encouraged to actively participate. Novelty matters in the world of porn, so audience members were recruited through the Internet but restricted to attending one shoot a year. I say audience members, but the members of the public who attended the shoot were actually performers. Our job was to play the role of an unruly and voyeuristic crowd for the real audience, the people who paid to watch a series called Public Disgrace on the Internet.

The venue of the shoot I attended, a bar called Showdown, was on a side street haunted by drug addicts and the mentally ill just south of the Tenderloin, next to a Vietnamese sandwich shop and a flophouse called the Winsor Hotel (REASONABLE RATES DAILY-WEEKLY). When I arrived, several people were standing at the entrance waiting to get in, including a group of young men and a straight couple in their thirties. We signed releases, showed our photo IDs, and a production assistant took a mug shot of each of us holding our driver's license next to our face. Then she gave us each two drink tickets that could be redeemed at the bar. "Depending on how wasted everyone seems to be I will give you more," she said.

That evening's performer, a diminutive blonde who went by the stage name Penny Pax, flew up to San Francisco from her home in Los Angeles especially for the Public Disgrace shoot. She had told Donna that one of the first pornos she ever watched was Public Disgrace, and since she got into the business herself she had been eager to make one. Her personal request for the evening was that Princess Donna attempt to anally fist her.

The bar was a narrow room that recalled a bygone San Francisco of working-class immigrants. Old-fashioned smoked-glass lamps hung over the wooden bar. A color-copied picture of Laura Palmer from David Lynch's television show *Twin Peaks* hung on the wall, next to a stopped clock with a fake bird's nest in the cavity where a pendulum should have been. A back room, dark and square, had black wallpaper patterned with alternating illustrations of two parrots on perches and a vase of flowers. The crew from Kink had rigged lighting overhead.

Princess Donna arrived with a small entourage, wearing a vacuum-tight black minidress that flattered her breasts. She is five foot seven with long, almost alarmingly thin limbs that make her look taller. She has large, brown, Bambi-ish eyes that, the night of the shoot, were complexly shadowed and wreathed in fake eyelashes, which Kink purchased in quantities of several hundred at a time. Her long brown hair was tied up in a high ponytail. She has a tattoo of an anatomically correct heart on her left shoulder and a cursive inscription that says *Daddy* on her inner right forearm. She strode into the room carrying a black vinyl purse from which a riding crop protruded. With her minidress she wore tan cowboy boots, which made the length of her legs appear heron-like. A neck bruise the size of a silver dollar that I had noticed during my first meeting with her a week before had faded.

Donna stood before the bar with the palindromically stage-named male performer, Ramon Nomar, surveying the room. He pointed up to several hooks on the ceiling and to a metal Juliet balcony over the bar. Donna nodded without a word. They retreated to the back. I asked a production assistant about the female performer. Penny Pax, she said, was having "quiet time."

Soon, the music was silenced (Kink had its own music, cleared for rights, to play). The bartender removed his gingham shirt and his tie and suddenly was wearing nothing but his waistcoat. Donna came out to make some announcements to the assembled crowd, which was well on its way to getting drunk.

"You might think we are doing things to the model that are mean or humiliating, but don't," said Donna. "She's signed an agreement." According to the agreement, the crowd had permission to poke the model, fondle her, and finger her, but only if they washed their hands and had neatly trimmed fingernails. A fingernail trimmer was available if necessary. "I'm going to be watching you like a hawk to make sure you're not doing degrading things to her pussy," Donna said. She continued: "You're allowed to spit on her chest but not her face. You can give her a hard spanking but you are not allowed to give her a hard smack." She pulled her production assistant over to her physically. "If Kat is the model"—here Kat bent over obligingly—"this would be a reasonable distance from which to spank her." Donna mimed responsible spanking practice.

The model, Donna went on to explain, could not leave the set bruised, because she had another shoot coming up that week. Therefore, Donna said, at some point she might have to forbid certain practices to ensure Penny's body remained unmarked.

Donna concluded her speech with a more theoretical exposition. The whole point of Public Disgrace, she explained, is that it's supposed to seem spontaneous, and that "you guys are not supposed to know that we're coming here." Taking video was forbidden, photographs with phones were fine, but the most important thing: "Don't ignore us. I'm going to walk her in with a sign that says 'I'm a worthless cunt.' So react to that." She repeated that nail clippers and files were available for anyone who wanted them and reminded the audience to wash their hands in the

bathroom before touching the model. Then she returned to the
back room.

A few minutes later Donna emerged with Penny Pax and Ramon in tow. Penny was small, just over five feet tall, with full
natural breasts, milky white skin, and a chin-length bob of corn-
silk blond. Her eyes were the rich azure of a blue raspberry Blow
Pop. She was very pretty, and decidedly not plastic or spray-tanned.
She looked like a model in a JCPenney catalog. She wore a denim
miniskirt, white high heels, and a white tank top. Donna looked
her over, then deftly pulled the straps of Penny's tank top off her
arms and folded them down. She turned Penny around, unhooked
her white bra, and tossed it to one side. From a black duffel bag
under a table Donna picked up and put back various coils of rope,
judging the weight and length of each one. Meanwhile, Ramon
stared—the only word for it is *lovingly*—at Penny's exposed breasts,
their stretch marks visible. Grabbing them, Donna executed a
complicated-looking tie, raising the breasts to bra elevation by
winding the rope around each one. She pulled the straps of Penny's
tank top back over her shoulders, then tied Penny's arms behind
her back.

"Look at that," said Donna, surveying her work and turning
Penny around. "You look gorgeous." Ramon stepped in and
looked Penny over with the tender carnivorousness of a dime-store
bodice ripper. He ran his hand over Penny's body from behind,
turned her around and examined her, kissed and inhaled her hair,
then put his hand up her skirt and began feeling her while staring
intently at her body. This was his way of preparing for the shoot.
Ramon was from Spain and had a sharp accent. He rarely smiled.
He wore a tight black T-shirt that showed off his impressive pec-
torals, black pants, and black combat boots. He was just over six
feet tall, tan, and sculpted like an Iberian Bruce Willis. This was
an attractive couple. Donna hung a sign, which indeed was I'M A

WORTHLESS CUNT, around Penny's neck, then grabbed Penny roughly by the hair and took her out the door.

Now the cameras were recording. Now we could redeem our drink tickets. The bar was full, mostly with men. These men I would divide into two groups: the openly slavering, confident about the righteousness of their lust, and the self-conscious, worried about breaking the taboos of touching and insulting a woman. They were joined by a smattering of females, some of whom were there with their boyfriends, others who had come together in pairs. Donna had exchanged her cowboy boots for patent leather high heels and now strode through the door purposefully, she and Ramon on either side of Penny, who looked up at her tall handlers with baleful blue eyes.

"Tell everybody why you're here," ordered Donna, as the people drinking at the bar feigned surprise. "I'm a worthless cunt!" said Penny. Using some kind of professional wrestling trick, Ramon lifted her up by her neck and sat her on the bar. Working together, Donna and Ramon stuffed a cocktail napkin in her mouth and taped it into a gag, taking turns slapping her on her face and her breasts. They ripped off her spotless white tank top. The rope had cut off circulation to Penny's breasts and they looked painfully swollen.

"Who wants to touch it!" asked Donna. "Who wants to play with this worthless little cunt?" The bar patrons obligingly hit, fingered, and spanked her. From her handbag, from which the riding crop still menacingly protruded, Donna now withdrew a device that crepitated with electric charges and started using it to shock Penny. Ramon removed what remained of Penny's clothes, then his belt, and began gently swiping it at Penny, who was soon pinioned on the floor.

"I thought it was your dream," goaded Donna. "I thought it was your dream to shoot for this site. You didn't come ready?"

She looked around the room. "What's her name?" she demanded. "Everyone knows what her name is."

"Worthless cunt!" yelled the crowd.

"What pretty girl wants to grab her titties?" A woman in attendance obliged. Ramon took off his pants, balancing on each foot as he pulled them over his combat boots. He was not wearing any underwear; his penis looked like the trunk of a palm tree. The bar patrons burst into applause.

He picked Penny up and had sex with her against the bar as the extras continued to smack at her breasts. Penny, still gagged, was wide-eyed. Her mascara had begun to run in rivers down her face. She had the option of halting everything with verbal and nonverbal cues but she did not exercise it. Suddenly, Donna stopped the show. "Everyone, I have an announcement," she said, as she removed the ropes still tied around Penny's breasts. "No more smacking this boob," she said, pointing to the right one, which had red marks on it. They resumed shooting.

Ramon, who had biceps like cannons, hoisted Penny around the room and the crowd followed, vying with one another for a good sight line. He was able to walk around holding Penny in one arm, wielding the zapper in the other. "Zap me!" requested a male audience member. Ramon rolled his eyes and did so without breaking rhythm. "Ouch," said the guy, looking sore. Ramon removed Penny's gag and guided her into a blow job, during which Penny theatrically gagged. Donna stood by, slapping and shocking, and then joined in. Using her hands, she made Penny ejaculate, to the delight of the crowd. After fifteen or twenty minutes, Donna called for a break.

Paused in the middle of his exertions, Ramon looked up at the ceiling with a look of super-intense concentration. Penny was on the floor. He picked her up and sat her on the bar. He and Donna tenderly tucked her hair back from her face and wiped off her sweat and the grime from the floor with Cottonelles. Donna, like a trainer during a boxing match, removed Penny's false eyelashes, gave her water, and kissed her on the cheek. During this reprieve from shooting, the crowd, which had been as verbally abusive as directed, acted sheepish.

"You are beautiful and I'd take you to meet my mother!" yelled one man who had been particularly enthusiastic about yelling "worthless cunt." Ramon asked for a drink. "What do you want?" said the bartender. "A soda," said Ramon. "Porno guy wants a soda!" echoed the loud man.

When shooting resumed, a female audience member, heavily tattooed and wearing a miniskirt and a ragged T-shirt that had two skeletal hands printed across her breasts, had a go at Penny's body. Things continued in this way for more than an hour. Chairs were knocked over. Drinks were spilled. The bartender had by now removed his vest and was shirtless. The crowd was drunk and excited, although not entirely unembarrassed. "Make that bitch choke," shouted the shouty man. Then: "Sorry!"

Donna began to wind things down. "OK, guys," she said, to prepare the audience, "the pot shot's not the end, though." The crowd cheered. With the cameras off, Ramon and Penny had vanilla missionary sex on a table to get to the point where he could ejaculate. He nodded when he was ready, then put Penny on the floor, and masturbated until he came on her face. Again the room burst into applause.

The performers took a break. Ramon's job was now done. With the room's attention focused on Penny he yanked off his sweaty T-shirt, flung it into a corner, and wandered off into a dark part of the bar, naked but for his combat boots. Like a long-distance runner who has just crossed the finish line, he walked it off, moving his arms in circles, wiping the sweat from his face with his arm, and taking deep breaths. Nobody noticed him.

Eventually he recovered his composure, toweled off, and put his black jeans back on. Penny, meanwhile, rested primly on a chair and sipped water. Her expression was, in a word, elated.

I joined Donna at the bar. What was going to happen next?

"I want to get my hand all the way in her ass," she said. "She's never done that before and she wants to try it."

Princess Donna sat Penny Pax down on a bar table. She had a Hitachi Magic Wand and a bottle of lubricant. "I need all the room that's in her holes for my hand," she announced, and the audience deferentially took a step back. After Donna accomplished her task, the crowd chanted, "Squirt, squirt, squirt, squirt," and then Penny did. I watched all this from a corner, standing next to Ramon, who had a towel around his bronzed shoulders and was drinking a bottle of pilsner.

Shooting was coming to a close. Donna and Ramon moved Penny back to the bar and strung her up by her wrists to the metal balcony. I saw Donna in a corner, carefully wiping down a beer bottle with a sanitizing wipe. And that was the final shot of the evening: Penny tied up and suspended from the railings of the balcony by her wrists, while a member of the audience penetrated her with a beer bottle. Ramon, now shirtless and in jeans, casually sparked the zapper across his pectoral muscles a couple of times, then reached out and zapped Penny on her tongue. Then it was done. With a debonair flourish, Ramon effortlessly picked up the tiny starlet and carried her out of the room in his arms.

Kink interviews its female performers before and after every shoot. It's a de-escalation strategy that reminds the viewer—if he watches to the end (Kink does not release the demographics of its audience, but studies have found that 95 percent of paid porn is watched by men)—of the controlled conditions of what he just watched, and confirms that the activity was consensual and that the model has recovered. Penny wandered out for her postgame interview wearing pink glasses, a gray bathrobe, and a pair of Uggs. But for her smeary mascara, she looked like a college student on her way to a dormitory bathroom. Donna arranged Penny's bathrobe to reveal her breasts. Other than that, like most postgame interviews with athletes, this one was a little bland.

DONNA
So, Penny, how did you enjoy the shoot this evening?

PENNY
I had a great time, it was amazing. There was so much going on.

HECKLING AUDIENCE MEMBER #1
I actually want to take you out for lunch later!

HECKLING AUDIENCE MEMBER #2
You have really pretty eyes!

DONNA
All right, everybody, hold on. Tell me what your favorite parts were.

PENNY
Probably, uh, just the getting handled by everyone and not really knowing how many hands were on me, or who was touching me . . . And then the—I don't know, did you get your fist in my butt?

DONNA
I did.

PENNY
Well, that was awesome. Yay! I can't wait to see it!

DONNA
Yeah, that was rad. Round of applause for the anal fisting!

[*Audience applauds.*]

DONNA
And you also said that you had never squirted like that before?

PENNY
Yeah, that was ridiculous. How did you do that?

DONNA
Magic fingers. Years of practice.

PENNY
Yeah, it was amazing.

DONNA
What were the most challenging parts?

PENNY
Uh, probably putting your fist in my butt? That was pretty challenging. It felt really full.

DONNA
On a scale of one to ten, how would you rate your happiness leaving the shoot?

PENNY
Eleven!

[*Applause. Whistles.*]

DONNA
So is it safe to say that you would come back and shoot for
the site again?

PENNY
Yes.

DONNA
Do you want a shower?

[*Penny Pax nods.*]

DONNA
Let's get you a shower!

MALE AUDIENCE MEMBER
A golden shower!

FEMALE AUDIENCE MEMBER
Can I come?

After this conclusion, Penny and I retreated to a stairwell
behind the bar. Penny, I learned, was twenty-three years old. I
asked if she had been working in the industry since she was eighteen. No, she said, she wished. She had been in the industry for
only six months. Before working in porn she was a lifeguard in

Fort Lauderdale. Being a lifeguard in Fort Lauderdale had been pretty boring. She had gone to San Fernando Valley and soon found representation from Mark Spiegler, who is one of the top agents in the business. He was known, I gathered, for representing performers who didn't play dumb and were willing to have anal sex. Penny wasn't dumb. I asked her about the shoot. I wanted to know how it had felt.

"It's a little uncomfortable in the beginning, for the anal," she said. (She was presumably referring to a moment early in the shoot when Ramon jumped up on the bar, stuffed a lemon in Penny's mouth, and had anal sex with her. "Nice boots, man!" someone in the audience yelled. Penny made a nonverbal cue to slow down and Donna jumped over and slathered her with lubricant.) "But my body warms up pretty quickly and then there's no discomfort." Slightly incredulous, I asked if there were moments of genuine pleasure. She looked at me like I was crazy. "Yeah. Like the whole thing! The whole thing." She apologized for not being more articulate and explained she was in a state of delirium. "We call it 'dick drunk,'" she said. "I'm a little dick drunk right now because it was just very nice." She looked at me. "You want to do something like that?" I tried to imagine a world where I would feel uninhibited enough to do what she had just done. It was impossible.

I rode back to the Mission in a van with Donna and Penny and Ramon. Penny and Ramon were both sleeping over at the landmarked Moorish castle that houses Kink. They said they usually worked in mainstream porn in the Valley, but enjoyed coming to San Francisco for the fetish jobs. In the shoot he was doing tomorrow for New Sensations in Los Angeles, Ramon lamented, they wouldn't even let him pull the girl's hair.

"In L.A. most of that doesn't require any bondage or much rough sex at all," explained Penny. "It's just, like, three positions.

We call them gonzo scenes. It's super-quick. When I do the gonzo scenes I usually don't get to have an orgasm. Here, at Kink, they're like, 'You're going to come.'" I gathered that for performers, making more extreme pornography was like being a writer's writer, where the value of the work was most apparent to other people immersed in the same field, and the respect one earned was of a different, more meaningful order than mainstream acclaim.

Over the course of the next several weeks I watched Princess Donna direct and star in more films. I watched her perform in a roller-derby-themed episode of a series called Fucking Machines where she wielded a drill retrofitted with a giant dildo. I watched her train for her new role as director of a Kink series called Ultimate Surrender, a girl-on-girl wrestling tournament. For three eight-minute rounds, two women wrestled each other. The goal was for one woman to pin the other and molest her for as long as possible. For the fourth round, the winner had sex with the loser wearing a strap-on dildo. It was one of Kink's most popular series and was sometimes shot before a live studio audience. Princess Donna also directed a series called Bound Gangbangs, and one day was inspired to do a shoot where all the men were dressed as pandas.

I was not sure what question I was trying to answer by watching the production of so much creative and exaggerated sex. The old question was whether one was "for" or "against" porn. This question had been unhelpful since 2005 if not earlier. Decisions about how porn should be obscured or banned in public spaces didn't matter in a time when watching porn was a question of typing some words into a search box while at home alone. It was impossible, in a democracy, to advocate for the censorship of all sexual activity on the Internet. One could draw up a list of crass gestures to which one was personally opposed, but parsing which kinds of sex were "good" or "bad" had resulted historically in the prohibition of gay sex, interracial sex, transgender sex, bisexuality, and literature about birth control and family planning. Not all porn was like the porn made at Kink, but when you set porn free, the simulation of violence and ritual public humiliation of a woman was what you got. You could refuse to watch it, but not watching porn offered no liberation from the anxieties caused by the other people in your life, or in the world, who watched it. Banning porn from your life also cut you off from the most comprehensive visual repository of sexual fantasy in human history, which had to have some value.

I, personally, was not having sex while all this was going on. Not that the sex I would've had, if I'd been having sex, would've been anything like the sex going on at the castle. The Kink actors were more like athletes or stuntmen and -women performing punishing feats, and part of what I admired was the ease with which they went in and out of it, the comfort with which they inhabited their bodies, their total self-assurance and sense of unity against those who condemned their practice. I possessed none of those qualities. I was, at that time, so miserable about being alone, and half-convinced by the logic that I could somehow solve the problem of loneliness by avoiding sex until I fell in love, that I was in the middle of a long and ultimately pointless stretch of celibacy.

The women at Kink came to porn for various reasons. Bobbi Starr, a twenty-nine-year-old who won the *Adult Video News* Female Performer of the Year award in 2012, was raised in a Pentecostal Christian family in San Jose, California, and was homeschooled until middle school. She trained as a swimmer, competed in the Junior Olympics, and earned a scholarship to study music at San Jose State University. She was twenty-two years old and working as a classical musician when she watched porn for the first time. Sitting down with a male friend, who was surprised at her lack of familiarity, she watched several videos, including one called *Bong Water Butt Babes*. Very little needs to be said about this video except that the bedroom set is covered in sheets of plastic. Starr was mesmerized and applied for a job at Kink. After getting hung upside down and sexually tortured in a tank of water, she signed with Mark Spiegler as her agent and moved to Los Angeles.

Lorelei Lee was nineteen and had just graduated from high school in San Diego when her boyfriend told her about a website called SoCal Co-eds. Lee posed sitting on a surfboard, lying across a washing machine, sitting at a desk with her feet up, and wearing a UC–Santa Barbara sweatshirt. To accompany the photos she recorded a voice-over. This was in 1999. She figured nobody would see the photos, because they were on the Internet, which nobody looked at. She did it for the money but even that first time it was not just for the money but also because it was "some kind of thrill." Her earnings from porn put her through college. She had an MFA in creative writing and met her husband at Kink, where he was a director.

Rain DeGrey described herself as a "24/7 lifestyle kinkster" and "pansexual." For years she had not admitted, to her partners and even to herself, that bondage and flogging turned her on. She knew that even in the Bay Area there were people who would judge her, but eventually she "came out as kinky." One day, she was tied up in her local dungeon, the Citadel, getting flogged by a friend, when someone suggested she try to do some of this stuff professionally.

Princess Donna grew up in Sacramento, where both her parents had worked in the medical industry. She went to college at New York University, where she signed up for a class in gender and sexuality theory, began reading Simone de Beauvoir and Judith Butler, and met her first girlfriend. On a break home in Sacramento, she went to a strip club and decided she wanted to try dancing at one. When an acquaintance mentioned that she was earning money by posing for photos for a BDSM website called Insex, Donna thought she might try out that, too.

Insex was founded in 1997 by Brent Scott, a former professor from Carnegie Mellon University who performed in his videos the role of handler, bondage rigger, and dominator under the name "PD." It was one of the earliest BDSM porn sites on the Internet, offering pre-broadband live feeds where viewers could interact and instruct the models via chat rooms. Donna had been promoted from modeling to torturing at Insex when she heard that there was an opening for a director at the Wired Pussy electricity fetish department at Kink. She sent in her résumé. In 2004, when she was twenty-two years old, Donna got the job and moved to San Francisco.

Some people said Kink was not "real" porn. Kink was thought of as different from San Fernando Valley porn because it was in Northern California, had many performers and directors who came to it from San Francisco's queer pornography scene, and because it consciously distanced itself from the stereotype of the industry as a group of exploitative lowlifes. It fashioned itself as a slightly unconventional tech company in a city of tech companies, offering its full-time employees catered lunches, retirement plans, and health insurance. Most San Fernando Valley pornographers didn't care to reassure viewers that the sex they watched had been consensual, but Kink videos were often preceded by a good fifteen minutes of backstage demystification, and not of the professional wrestling fake-reality kind. Kink emphasized consent, they wanted real orgasms, they followed the safeguards honed in San Francisco's long-established BDSM scene, they bought lubricant by the barrel (literally: they had blue plastic barrels of lube in the basement). Insofar as was possible in an industry where the employees took physical and psychological risks, they tried to give a clean conscience to consumers of raunchy porn. That did not mean they always succeeded: in 2014 and 2015 there were four lawsuits filed by performers claiming Kink failed to protect their health and safety on set, including two actors, a couple in real life, who claimed to have contracted HIV on the set of Princess Donna's Public Disgrace, an allegation that Kink has denied. As far as is known, the lawsuits are still pending with no resolution of the charges.

The company's self-described mission to "demystify alternative sexuality" and its woman-centric presentation—the Bound Gangbangs series was advertised as "women explore their darkest fantasies"—meant that perhaps more performers at Kink came from nice families or had college degrees, but not everyone had supportive parents or explained their sexuality with references to Judith Butler. I asked one performer, Ashli Orion, why she had a tattoo that said, "Shoot Frank." "Frank's my dad's name," she said. She giggled. "I have daddy issues. I hate my dad. But it's also from *Donnie Darko*. That's what I tell people. Not many people know my dad's name is Frank."

I didn't inquire further. Lorelei Lee, who had a happy childhood, had said something with the evident weariness of someone regularly asked to explain herself: "If you look at people in porn as a group, you might find a lot of people who do not have strong family connections, and in some ways that can make it easier to choose to do something that is looked down on by a lot of people," she said. "If nobody's making rules for you, you have to make up your own rules."

The porn at Kink made you think about rules. Rules, in particular, about what the sexual fantasies of a moral person should
look like. Legal rules were one thing, and personal rules were
another. Some experiences you avoid not because you know you
don't like them but because you don't want to like them. I had
never tried masturbating to porn on my computer. I associated my
computer with labor, boredom, and abjection. I associated porn
with a man grabbing a woman's lower jaw to force her gaze in his
direction, or slapping her face as if to keep her from slipping into
unconsciousness, or with ads selling "cum-craving sluts." With
friends I had tested out several other explanations for why I
didn't watch porn. I had said I thought the idea of masturbating
"to" something was an imposition of masculine ideas of sexuality. I had wondered aloud if women weren't stimulated by images
but rather by ineffable gestures and olfactory chemicals.

Of the 21.2 billion visits to Porn Hub in 2015, data analytics
identified about 24 percent as female and 76 percent male. A lot of
theories were floated on the subject of why so many women didn't
like watching porn. Most of them fell into one of three arguments:

1. Women did not watch visual porn in equivalent numbers
   to men because the images were the wrong images.
2. Women were not physically "wired" to respond to visual
   stimulation and preferred to fantasize with novels or stories.
3. Women had simply suppressed, through cultural
   conditioning, some vital part of their sexual psyche.

And yet:

1. There were a lot of images to choose from.
2. Thinking of an aversion to porn as a biological preference
   was easier, perhaps, than having to wade through fantasies

like "tiny teen snatched up and fucked in van," and
"stepdaughter fucked by pervert dad."

3. Not wanting to click on a link that said "hardcore lesbian
   scissoring" and touch myself didn't mean I was repressed.

Or?

I started to think about the origins of my rules.

Deep Throat, which came out in 1972, was the first (and possibly
the last) pornographic film that American women watched in
significant numbers. The film was made for $25,000. It grossed
tens of millions in ticket sales. It remains an artifact of a singular
moment in time, when a lot of Americans had rejected the religious prohibitions against porn but had yet to hear about the
feminist ones. Both *Time* and *Newsweek* ran cover stories about
its star, Linda Lovelace. The film received reviews in mainstream
publications such as *The New York Times*. Even the feminist publication *Off Our Backs* dispatched a reviewer, Christine Stansell,
who attended a screening with a male friend.

"There was none of the male sadism and negation of female
sexuality which I had predicted," wrote Stansell in her review.
"But this intellectual understanding of the quality of degradation
fails to account for the most significant aspect of the film for me:
the fact that I freaked out." She spent most of the film in the bathroom, "to minimize the feminist martyr aspect of it all." She
concluded that *Deep Throat* was symptomatic of "a culture which
sucks emotion out of sex and sensuality out of our bodies and
turns the whole business into a hot-dog stuffed in a Wonder Bread
bun." And soon a new kind of moral objection to porn found articulation: the feminist one.

The anti-porn feminist movement began with protests of

depictions of violence against women. The movement was galvanized in 1975 by a slasher film called *Snuff*, which claimed (falsely) to show the real rape and dismemberment of a woman. A year later, more women protested when a Rolling Stones billboard on Sunset Boulevard in Los Angeles showed a bruised woman tied up in a chair next to the words "I'm 'Black and Blue' from the Rolling Stones—and I love it." Images like these made women feel like lesser citizens of the world. The feminists proposed a vocabulary with which to express this dismay—words like *exploitation, objectification, misogyny, degradation*. They showed how these images fit into larger patterns of structural inequality and violence. Today, if I were to explain what is wrong with the 1978 cover image from *Hustler* of a woman's leg being shoved into a meat grinder, I would use the language of feminism to argue that violence against women is a tool of patriarchal control, and that the commercial exploitation of violence against women informs the ideological foundation of their continued oppression.

The movement shifted from boycotts of violent images to boycotting porn with the idea, as Andrea Dworkin wrote, that porn "conditions, trains, educates, and inspires men to despise women, to use women, to hurt women." Susan Brownmiller called pornography "the undiluted essence of antifemale propaganda." The feminists dissected the politics of sexual stimulation. They articulated what might be demeaning and servile about women dressed up in bunny costumes. They taught men that women were not in the office to be groped. They explained that a woman with a clitoris in her throat was a self-serving male fantasy.

"There can be no 'equality' in porn, no female equivalent, no turning the tables in the name of bawdy fun," wrote Brownmiller in 1975. "Pornography, like rape, is a male invention, designed to dehumanize women, to reduce the female to an object of sexual access, not to free sensuality from moralistic or parental inhibition." In 1978, the first feminist anti-pornography conference in San Francisco culminated in a march around a cluster of porn shops on Broadway. The protest included a float plastered with pictures of porn as well as a statue of a bride, dozens of lit candles, and a lamb carcass smeared with blood and red feathers. The concept, according to *Off Our Backs*, was "to convey the theme of the oppression of women through the images of madonna/whore."

A legal strategy followed. In 1980, Linda Lovelace, the star of *Deep Throat*, published her memoir *Ordeal* under her given name of Linda Boreman. In the book Boreman alleged she had acted in pornographic films only under the threat of abuse from her husband, Chuck Traynor. She would later testify to the Meese Commission that "every time someone watches that movie they're watching me being raped." Anti-porn feminists including Andrea Dworkin, Catherine MacKinnon, and Gloria Steinem flocked to her aid, investigating the feasibility of a lawsuit, but the statute of limitations had passed. In 1983, Dworkin and MacKinnon, who were both then teaching at the University of Minnesota, drafted what they called a "Model Antipornography Civil Rights Ordinance" that claimed as its legal legitimacy that "pornography is an act of sex discrimination." Activists in Minneapolis, where anti-porn feminists had taken to occupying sex shops and surrounding the men browsing the video racks, succeeded in bringing the ordinance to the city council, where it passed, only to be vetoed by the mayor, who said that it violated the First Amendment. When a version of the ordinance succeeded in Indianapolis, the courts determined that it did, in fact, violate the First Amendment. There the feminist legal challenge to pornography expired.

Today, because porn has triumphed, anti-porn feminism is thought of as a failed movement. I would say this isn't true.

Anti-porn feminism might not have done much to temper the explosion of pornography in the video age but it deeply affected the way some people, perhaps especially some women, felt about what they were watching. Catherine MacKinnon's statement that "porn is the theory; rape is the practice" was a glib overgeneralization, but the idea lives on that porn is a theory that has negative effects on the practice of sexuality. The radical ideas of the movement filtered down into popular culture as a series of moral arguments against porn that social liberals could accept. These were the notions that I had inherited, that had made me wary of porn: that porn by definition was oriented toward the sexual desires of men; that it therefore offered few positive experiences for women; that it objectified and racialized women's bodies and glorified sexual violence. From the earliest days in which feminism turned its eye to porn, it became acceptable to make the distinctly unfeminist assumption that the women involved in porn were unconsciously complicit in their own exploitation. Porn performers were victims: they were traumatized by childhood abuse, forced into their jobs by abusive men, or abusers of substances themselves. This did not go unnoticed by the performers. When *Ms.* magazine convened a panel on pornography in New York in 1978—a panel that neglected to include anybody who worked in the industry—the porn stars Gloria Leonard, Annie Sprinkle, and Marlene Willoughby stood outside holding signs that read "I Am Not a Female Captive" and "Ms. Exploits Sex Too!" (One poster showed an issue of *Ms.* with the cover line "Erotica and Pornography: Do You Know the Difference?")

Anti-porn feminism created another problem. What did "feminist" sex look like? If a feminist felt sexually stimulated while watching *Deep Throat*, would she compromise a more eq-

uitable future by enjoying it? "Porn" means only material produced with the intention of inciting a sexual response over an
aesthetic or emotional one. What is pornographic is therefore a
highly subjective experience. What inspires sexual feelings in one
person might provoke disgust or boredom in another. If pornography was inherently masculine, "an act of sex discrimination,"
were the sexual desires of "women" therefore impossible to visu-
alize? Did they resist representation and articulation? Soon another wing of the feminist movement, grouped under the label of
"pro-sex" or "sex positive" feminism, emerged to address some
of these questions.

"When I first heard there was a feminist movement against
pornography, I twitched," wrote Ellen Willis in her 1979 *Village
Voice* essay "Feminism, Moralism, and Pornography":

> For obvious political and cultural reasons, nearly all porn is sex-
> ist in that it is the product of a male imagination and aimed at a
> male market; women are less likely to be consciously interested
> in pornography, or to indulge that interest, or find porn that
> turns them on. But anyone who thinks women are indifferent to
> pornography has never watched a bunch of adolescent girls pass
> around a trashy novel. Over the years I've enjoyed various pieces
> of pornography—some of them of the sleazy Forty Second Street
> paperback sort—and so have most women I know. Fantasy, after
> all, is more flexible than reality, and women have learned, as a
> matter of survival, to be adept at shaping male fantasies to their
> own purposes. If feminists define pornography, per se, as the
> enemy, the result will be to make a lot of women ashamed of
> their sexual feelings and afraid to be honest about them. And
> the last thing women need is more sexual shame, guilt, and
> hypocrisy—this time served up as feminism.

Willis criticized the attempts of anti-porn feminists to distinguish between "pornography" (bad for women) and "erotica" (good for women). She wrote that the binary tended to devolve into "What turns me on is erotic; what turns you on is pornographic." In these early years of anti-porn feminism a pattern emerged, where what was envisioned as "feminist" sex tended away from literal descriptions of physical activity. Andrea Dworkin's *Intercourse* is an extreme but lasting example—her assertion that women want "a more diffuse and tender sensuality that involves the whole body and a polymorphous tenderness." One theorist Dworkin quoted pictured a possible future of sex without thrusting. Instead, sex would be like "a stream that meets another stream," and "a more mutual lying together."

Other feminists responded to the feminist porn wars by making porn. In response to the anti-porn polemics in *Off Our Backs*, a group of women began publishing *On Our Backs* in 1984. Billed as "Entertainment for the Adventurous Lesbian," the magazine soon expanded from print to include Fatale, a line of pornographic videos aimed at the lesbian market. Another direct response came from women who had worked for years in the industry, who began speaking and writing about their experiences with porn, responding to the claims about their exploitation, and directing their own films. The Golden Age film stars did not all have Linda Lovelace's story of exploitation, although Linda Lovelace remains the archetypal tragic victim of porn in the national imagination. Some found their way to porn via the utopian ideas of the counterculture, others by the usual accidents that shape people's destinies.

Annie Sprinkle came to sex work by way of a hippie adolescence. After dropping out of the artists' commune in Oracle, Arizona, at the age of seventeen, she got a job answering phones at an erotic massage parlor, then began giving erotic massages and sometimes having sex with her customers. It was 1973, and Sprinkle had a hippie's view of sex as a natural and abundant gift to celebrate and share.

Sprinkle moved to New York after starting an affair with Gerard Damiano, the director of *Deep Throat*, whom she met when he came to Tucson to testify in an obscenity trial. In New York she began working at the Spartacus Spa in Midtown, and then found her own way to porn. Her first starring role was in a film called *Teenage Deviate*, where she performed under the stage name of "Annie Sprinkles" (her given name was Ellen Steinberg).

At eighteen, Annie Sprinkle (as her name was later shortened) had bobbed brown hair, full breasts, and a twinkly smile. As a performer, she affected the airy grooviness of the hippie she once was, with a wry sense of humor coming through. As the 1970s progressed she came to be known as one of the performers most willing to try controversial sex acts. She peed on men, fisted them with Crisco, and even vomited on one (using, she later revealed, canned soup). She held the hand of another performer during what might be the first clitoral piercing in porn. After performing in more than a hundred movies directed by men, she directed one herself. *Deep Inside Annie Sprinkle* was the second-highest-grossing X-rated feature in 1982.

In 1983, Sprinkle began hosting a support group for performers who were now leaving the industry. Its members were Sprinkle, Gloria Leonard, Veronica Vera, Candida Royalle, and Jane Hamilton (who acted as Veronica Hart). They called the group Club 90, for the address of Sprinkle's apartment on Lexington Avenue. All five would put their sexual experience in pornography toward other professions: Vera founded a cross-dressing academy, Miss Vera's Finishing School for Boys Who Want to Be Girls; Gloria Leonard was the first president of the Free Speech Coalition, which advocated for the First Amendment rights of the industry; Hamilton went on to work as a porn director and later an executive at VCA, a major Southern California production company. In 1984, Candida Royalle produced Femme, a series of videos marketed to women and couples.

Rites of Passion, Annie Sprinkle's 1984 collaboration with Candida Royalle about tantric sex, is typical of Femme's style: soft-focus video and women with teased hairstyles explaining their sexual dilemmas. Jeanna Fine plays a young woman increasingly dissatisfied with her lovers. She has unfulfilling sex with an uncaring bodybuilder type, then expresses her frustration and asks him to leave (he does, in a huff). Afterward, she sits alone in her apartment in an armchair next to a pseudo–Georgia O'Keeffe painting hanging on one wall.

"In my search I tried everything," she says of her failure to find sexual satisfaction. "Every type of man, every type of woman. I tried it everywhere, from on airplanes to on the subway at rush hour. Threesomes, orgies; I even tried"—here she pauses—"monogamy." Her despondence deepens. "Maybe I should just become celibate and forget the whole thing."

Then she meets her long-haired tantric lover. They have tantric sex over animated backdrops of autumn leaves and lotus flowers. "I returned to the place where I existed right from the start, where spirit meets flesh," she says. "We were the universal life force."

Sprinkle wanted to depict climax with something other than a cum shot on the face, so her heroine's orgasm is represented by an explosion of early-1980s computer effects with a roiling saxophone accompaniment. "I borrowed a special effect from *Star Trek*," Sprinkle said, in the autobiographical *Annie Sprinkle's Herstory of Porn*, of her attempt to create "the feeling of a cosmic orgasm of love."

As the years progressed, Sprinkle's porn did, too. She has described herself as "metamorphosexual." She invented a genre she called "docu-porn" and in 1991 directed and starred in *Linda/Les and Annie: A Female–Male Transsexual Love Story*, the first porn with a surgically constructed penis. She performed in art-porn movies like Nick Zedd's *War Is Menstrual Envy* and played the role of God in Cynthia Roberts's 1996 "feminist sex fantasy" *Bubbles Galore*. She made performance art, most famously with "Public Cervix Announcement," in which she inserted a speculum and invited the audience to inspect her cervix with a flashlight. Today she identifies as eco-sexual, which means she finds sexual stimulation in nature. She told me that there is even a culture of sadomasochism in eco-sexuality: people who might, for example, run naked through a field of nettles.

Annie Sprinkle explored sexual possibilities that would become familiar to the mainstream only decades later. What was, in the 1980s and 1990s, the future of sexuality was not really found in the pages of *Ms.*, but rather in the fringes of the pornographic, in the work of people like Sprinkle, who used pornography to explore their physical and psychological limits, to identify unconventional forms of sexual stimulation, and to question the gender binary. If the future was to be defined by a more honest and nuanced sexual culture, one in which sexual diversity was valued, the people with maximalist ambitions were futurists, and they had knowledge unavailable to those who had not considered their extremes. A better sexuality, if such a thing were possible, would be discovered by people who explored the widest range of sexual practice, not those who treated it as resistant to literal representation. I valued the ideas of feminism that spoke of liberating feminine sexuality from masculine ideas of sexiness, but it was as if, having cleaned out the clutter of masculine pornographic language and imagery, the only inoffensive concept left was a spartan white room dotted with patches of sunlight, starched curtains gently blowing from the open floor-to-ceiling windows.

This was either the empty canvas of the liberated sexual imagination or evidence of a deep aversion to physical reality, where any image of sex provoked disgust and had to be replaced with an innocuous interior design concept.

Today, marketing of porn intended to appeal to women often emphasizes producers' "tasteful," "natural," or "romantic" aesthetic. Or it appears under the *Cosmo*-inspired alibi of education and self-improvement, such as the genre of "guide pornos" that present themselves as how-to workshops on having better anal sex or giving a better blow job. It shrouds sexual stimulation in stories of dating, personal confession, self-help, romantic intrigue, and education. One self-described feminist video I watched had as its plot a woman turned on by watching a man assemble IKEA furniture. Another, *Marriage 2.0*, which won Movie of the Year at the Feminist Porn Awards, had long scenes of couples discussing the politics of their open relationships and a cameo by Christopher Ryan, the co-author of *Sex at Dawn*. These videos offered worthwhile romantic and educational entertainment, but did they inspire masturbation? In the marketing of these movies, the sex itself was not emphasized, the way it was on the online porn tubes. The video *I Fucking Love IKEA*, for example, which was directed by Erika Lust, was not described as "ripped carpenter bro cock fucks the shit out of insatiable busty rich girl" but rather, "I have a thing for IKEA (I know, it's weird), but making him buy and build stuff for me turns me on."

The pornographers at Kink, feminists themselves, had thrown all of this perceived self-censorship and sensitivity in the trash, along with the notion that feminine sex was a delicate, unnamable mystery. The rage and misogyny of the American male is an astonishing thing, its own natural wonder, like a geyser in a national park. But it had taken feminism to explain how the gagging, slapping, and sneering of porn might be hateful to women, and feminism to enhance its taboo. You couldn't have nun porn without Catholicism. You couldn't have Public Disgrace without feminism.

But I preferred the white cube. For years after watching the pornography shoots at Kink I still thought of myself as personally uninterested in porn. Instead of watching porn I read articles with titles like "Why Women Don't Like Porn." I read interviews with Stoya or Joanna Angel or Nina Hartley in *Cosmo* about why they made porn. I had interviewed Princess Donna, and watched her make porn. I still didn't go on xHamster and watch videos and masturbate to them. Googling "tiny blonde tied up and ass fucked in public" will lead you to a video I saw recorded in San Francisco one April evening. In life, the sex I saw there did not upset me, but when I came to the video via Google I wanted to turn it off.

My aversion to pornography was not because the images didn't stimulate, but because I did not want to be turned on by sex that was not the kind of sex I wanted to have. I knew I shared this feeling with certain Christians, certain feminists, and many people who could only articulate an uneasiness that fell outside of an ideology. I remained at least half-persuaded by the argument that a woman watched or made porn only as a member of a subordinate group trying to win the acceptance of the dominant group by conforming to its standards of sexuality and beauty. Nobody at the feminist sex shop suggested that the way to maximize pleasure was to go online and masturbate while watching "bondage slut gets a rough gangbang," which is what I finally did one day.

I was honestly surprised that it worked. It usually took me a long time to give myself an orgasm without a vibrator. I only had to watch the video for ten minutes. I started looking at porn on a semiregular basis, maybe once a month, when I was alone, had no prospects for sex, and didn't have a vibrator with me. The site indexes were useless, since I didn't have a particular fetish. I would click through until I found something that didn't annoy or upset me. I liked porn that had both masculine and feminine characters. It had to have a woman, and it had to have dicks. If a dick was a strap-on it had to be on a masculine-looking person, but she did not have to be a biological man. I didn't need and felt bored by setups, stories, character-specific fantasies, "talking dirty." I disliked the index terms. I wished, for example, that the "gang bang" category had a different, less aggressive name, like "group sex with >1 dick" and that a MILF ("Mom I'd Like to Fuck") was "woman >30." The industry's tendency to reduce people to the most offensive stereotypes of their age, race, ethnicity, body type, or gender seemed entirely unnecessary, although a friend of mine argued that the point of the language was to demarcate fantasy, just as in *Star Wars* the light saber was not called a "laser sword." So, on the Hot Guys Fuck channel, I watched porn advertising "big dumb Chad" or "tattoo stud Blake," and, on For Her Tube, browsed through the Doctor Tube, the Office Tube, and the Seduce Tube.

I had once thought of porn as a male-dominated force that standardized sexual expectations, and that it therefore imposed its will on my sexuality, but I saw that porn defied standardization. Some men clearly watched porn to experience a feeling of domination and control over women, and a lot of porn played to these fantasies. This fantasy of control transcended porn into an evident belief that masturbating to someone, or casting sexual judgment on her, was an expression of power over her. A common choice of insult by disdainful men on Internet comment threads was to say that they masturbated to some piece of content made by a woman with serious intent. I don't know why, but knowing porn as he does diminishes the specter of the leering man. You invade his temple, his redoubt. You have felt what he feels but you have felt it in your own way.

Watching porn left me more confident about my body. The "sexiness" used to sell clothes or toothpaste was very different from the sexiness that incited actual sex. Porn represented a wilderness beyond the gleaming edge of the corporate Internet and the matchstick bodies and glossy manes of network television. Porn had body hair, tattoos, assholes, bodily fluids, genitals, Mexican wrestling masks, birthday cake, ski goggles. The index entries on the most fetish-specific sites included "big clit," "chubby," "puffy nipples," "farting," "hairy pussy," "aged," "9 months pregnant," "short hair," "small tits," "muscled girl," "fat mature," and "ugly." In looking through all this I found unexpected reassurance that somebody will always want to have sex with me. This was the opposite of the long road toward sexual obsolescence that I had been taught to expect.

Because porn was a tour of human sexual diversity, I also watched porn that didn't really turn me on but that interested me as an exploration of the human body and what it looked like and what it could do. The experimental work made by Sprinkle was a more artsy example of this kind of porn, but it also happened in more commercial porn, often under the direction of women. If there were differences between porn made by men and porn made by women, it might be that the feminine aesthetic was less literal, showed a wider variation in stimuli, and tended to have costumes and fantasies that had nothing to do with the traditional repertoire of nurses, babysitters, and stepmoms. Porn made by women tended to be a little more bizarre, as I realized when I started to watch the work of Belladonna, who retired in 2012 but was probably the most influential pornographer for the current generation of women making porn. The directors at Kink spoke of her with reverence, as did many other directors in the industry.

Belladonna's non-porno name was Michelle Sinclair. She was born in 1981 in Biloxi, Mississippi, and raised in Utah. She started making porn after working at a strip club in Salt Lake City called American Bush. She became famous in 2003, when ABC's *Primetime* aired a documentary about what it was like to be a naive young woman in the industry. "Inside the new world of pornography," said a severe Diane Sawyer. "Be there as an eighteen-year-old makes a decision she can never take back." San Fernando Valley could not have pitched it better. A few years later Belladonna was a star performer and perhaps the most successful female director of hardcore pornography in the industry. For years she was the only female director under contract at the giant Valley studio Evil Angel. She had a franchise of more than eighty DVDs, many of them made with her then-husband, Aidan Riley, including seven installments of Belladonna's Fucking Girls, and ten chapters of Fetish Fanatics.

Belladonna, like Annie Sprinkle, seemed metamorphosexual. She had a round face and a gap-toothed smile. She occasionally performed with her head shaved and her underarms hairy. Her body was athletic. She made every kind of porn, including some of the most intense and violent porn I had seen, but it wasn't the sex that upset me the most. I had trouble watching *Manhandled 4*, where in the lead-up to the sex Ramon Nomar plays the jealous and abusive boyfriend all too convincingly, and slaps Belladonna for having looked at another guy. In addition to double penetration, peeing, deep throating, gagging, and begging, Belladonna also made porn about two people waking up in bed together and having vanilla sex. She made foot-fetish porn and sex-toy porn. She made porn with scenarios removed from any power dynamic I could try to impose on it, because it was porn between women wearing bunny heads. She made porn where she instructed how to give an enema, where she wore a surgical mask, or carnival face paint, or a vinyl outfit with pigtails, or where she played Dance Dance Revolution. She made porn when she was pregnant. She made a movie called *Cvrbongirl*, described by Evil Angel as "the fantasy of Belladonna as the 'Doll Maker,' a cross between Pinocchio's Gepetto, the Wizard of Oz, and a perverted Doctor Frankenstein, bringing dolls to life in her workshop so they can engage in lesbian depravity with each other." She made porn about a glory hole, where "the backdrop is a perfectly disgusting bathroom with rotting tile, a grimy floor, and numerous duct-tape-reinforced holes to serve as entry points." She made *Dirty Panties*, where "the director's cast of lovelies enjoys the powerful aroma that emanates from a woman's moist butt crack." Her own contribution to the genre of guide pornos, the ironic *Belladonna's How to Fuck*, includes the aforementioned enema, and a blow job during which the man pinches her nose as she goes down on him. She has performed in porn with people of many races and gender identifications, including in *Strapped Dykes*, parts one and two, and *Transsexual Playground*.

Now she has retired, to focus on motherhood and other projects. I watched a Vice documentary where she drank green juice and performed circus acrobatics on long swathes of silk hung from scaffolding. It was a strange moment when she appeared unexpectedly in Paul Thomas Anderson's film adaptation of *Inherent Vice*, the novel by Thomas Pynchon. Of all the cameos mentioned in reviews of the film that I had read, nobody had mentioned hers. I wondered what percentage of the audience recognized her, and whether they also had the feeling they knew her far more intimately than they knew Joaquin Phoenix, her counterpart on screen. I later read that she had turned down a larger role in the film because she now refused to perform nude.

Belladonna had moved on, but there was still Dana Vespoli, another director with Evil Angel, who has described the porn she directs as "psychosexual." Vespoli was born in 1972, and is known for her authenticity ("A tampon string hangs from her vagina as James fucks her asshole!" read the description of *Dana Vespoli's Real Sex Diary*). Her movies have included a send-up about ride-sharing called *Screwber X*. There was Joanna Angel, the self-described "punk rock porn princess." There was Jacky St. James, the director under contract with New Sensations who was inspired to make a BDSM video called *The Submission of Emma Marx* after finding the bestselling erotic novel *Fifty Shades of Grey*, in her words, "so incredibly weak and pathetic." Kimberly Kane, who directed for Vivid, was famous for having said, "If I had a cock, I'd be in jail." Sinnamon Love confronted taboos about shooting BDSM porn as a black performer. The enigmatic Mason, who has directed more than 140 hardcore gonzo films in which she stars only as a goading voice from behind the camera, appeared for years at industry events wearing a burka. In her 2004 movie *Riot Sluts* women smash the windows of a car with metal pipes in between sex scenes.

The pornography we have now is either the nadir of human civilization or it's pushing the boundaries of human experience. The protagonists of this pornography are not Hugh Hefner, founder of *Playboy*, or Al Goldstein, publisher of *Screw*, but the women who successfully captivate and monetize their online audiences. Porn taught me that the feminine expression of sexuality did not have to be a dildo in the shape of a dolphin to shed the vestiges of the patriarchy. It gave me an internal answer to the accusation of false consciousness that accompanied so much expression of sexuality by a woman. I knew I wasn't trying to inhabit the masculine if the force that guided my sexual decisions came from a physical feeling in my body. Figuring out what I liked in porn was like having my fortune told. It wasn't real, but it offered orientation.

The panda gang bang took place deep in the basement of the Kink armory, where rivulets of the long-suffocated Mission Creek still traced a path between moisture-eaten columns, and the air hung heavy with a stony dampness. On the day of the shoot, warm light glowed in the center of a cavernously empty space. Bathed in this glow, Ashli lay sleeping, impervious to the dark immensity of her surroundings. Her sleek black hair was draped over her shoulder; a small silken bow of the palest pink pinned it away from her face into a girlish side part. The hem of her pink dotted swiss dress had been carefully arranged to reveal a glimpse of her upper thigh through the gauze. On her feet she wore six-inch patent leather high heels embellished with lace. She slumbered on a bed of green leaves in a simulated bamboo forest beneath wraiths of mist produced by a Rosco Hazemaker puffing away beyond the circle of light, the sound of which did not disturb her.

The pandas approached her from behind. They waved their horrible paws and sniffed inquisitively. One stood over her, nibbling at a frond of bamboo. Another gently stroked her hair.

"Now poke her or kick her," ordered Donna from the darkness. The pandas fell upon her. The sound of ripping gauze and a snapped bra strap broke the quiet. They fondled and slapped at her now-exposed breasts. She awoke and screamed in fear. "But I love pandas, I love pandas!" she cried out.

The panda shoot was a taxing one. Donna hovered around the bears, using metal clamps to keep the furry folds of their costumes from hiding the action. They took turns with Ashli without conferring much. Finally the pandas retired to their bamboo bowers and the shoot was over.

LIVE WEBCAMS

On the computer a woman in north Florida was talking about the wildlife down where she's from. "Raccoons, possums, armadillos, moles," she listed. "Rattlesnakes, copperheads, water moccasins." She paused to think. "Black snakes, but they're not so bad." Her profile said she was born in 1959. Her blond-gray hair was long. She was topless, with ample, sagging breasts and a stomach tattoo of Yosemite Sam drawing his guns. On her lap was a large, two-headed dildo. "They've got those big-ass pythons in the Everglades," she said. "They're breeding with the water moccasins and they're creating a supersnake, y'all."

In Virginia, three men lay draped over one another in a bed, fund-raising with an aggressive strategy of languid bared-torso napping. They had promised a show when they received 775 tokens from their audience, from which they would receive $38.75 in earnings. Their audience discussed in the chat column on the right whether they would actually perform if they met their goal. "Nah, they too tired," someone wrote. They looked pretty tired.

In Denver, a plump, bespectacled woman spooned cupcake batter into a tin. She said she was eighteen and still a virgin. She was naked under her apron, and she promised to show her breasts as soon as she got the cupcakes in the oven. In Austria, a woman with a beehive, blue fingernail polish, and a polka-dotted bra gave her boyfriend the most halfhearted blow job in human history. He was wearing a turtleneck sweater but no pants. In Montreal, a woman with fuchsia hair penetrated herself with a toy light saber. A woman with a thin black ribbon tied around her neck in a bow, who gave her location as "Orgrimmar, Azeroth," a town from the computer game World of Warcraft, talked about the hardware she had in her computer. She nibbled a Burrito Bowl from Chipotle, slurped from a can of Mountain Dew, and showed off her pierced nipples for an audience of 1,150 people. In another chat room, 3,756 people watched as a stark-naked twenty-one-year-old with no makeup and a body like a juice guru performed a yoga routine in a day-lit room with creamy wall-to-wall carpeting, a Pilates ball in a corner behind her. She eased into a headstand.

For the first few weeks after I started watching Chaturbate, these were some of the people I watched. Chaturbate was a live webcam site that launched in 2011. It distinguished itself from the many other live webcam sites on the Internet by its democratic approach. It was free to watch—really free, as in no logging in or setting up passwords—and open to everyone of legal age. Its tabs offered live feeds of Females, Males, Couples, and Transsexuals. To start broadcasting, a person had only to register a name and beam herself to the world, eating Chipotle. Total sexual anarchy was forestalled by a zealous volunteer police force of users, who operated along the lines of Wikipedia moderators, reporting and shutting down any performers who looked suspiciously underage or who broke one of Chaturbate's few rules—the usual bans on violence, animals, and excrement.

A lot of the performers used the site to make money. Viewers could tip their favorite performers with tokens, Chaturbate's official currency. Chaturbate took a 50 percent cut, such that each token cost ten cents for the person who bought it and was worth five cents to the person who earned it. In exchange for some tokens, the performers might fulfill a request, or address the tipper directly. Despite this payment system, Chaturbate's freedom extended to impecunious viewers, who did not have to limit their participation to voyeurism but could also write jokes in the sidebar that made a performer giggle or, less generously, that insulted her. Performers chose dedicated audience members to moderate their rooms. The "mods" silenced misbehaving or mean-spirited viewers, or fund-raised while the performer spanked herself, tied her hand to a bedpost, or was otherwise occupied.

Beyond its lack of restrictions, it took a while to figure out what made Chaturbate special. At first glance, it was simply a framed box of amateur peep show performers determined to outdo one another in mimicking the costumes and attitudes of mainstream porn. The matrix of webcams that loaded on the homepage looked like most other adult webcam sites, which was to say that it provided an overwhelmingly gynecological perspective of the world. In the sidebars where viewers chatted with each other, it was still mostly men telling women they wanted to ejaculate on various parts of their bodies, or seeking individual attention from them, or telling them to do certain things or hold certain positions, and the women flattering and cooing in return. The porno gifs bounced annoyingly as ever in the margins; and the homepage's checkerboard of thumbnail images merged into a single disingenuous orgasm.

At first I avoided the most sexually explicit channels. I preferred to watch women, but not usually at their most pornographic. I watched when they were just doing things, chatting or cutting out paper hearts for Valentine's Day or listening to the songs of Miley Cyrus. I watched the women because they were more interesting than the men, who invariably positioned themselves in a black computer chair at a desk in ghastly desk-lamp illumination, dick in hand, making the usual motions, unless they reclined in bed and did the same, with little in the way of creativity or gimmicks. It was amazing, the diversity of what men wanted performed for them and how little they offered to others, except for a few of the gay guys, who understood that some form of flirtation might exhilarate the spirit and therefore did yoga routines in bike shorts or lip-synched to pop hits. I watched plenty of women and followed a few couples but I almost never bothered to click on the tab marked "Males" except when it was gay guys actually doing things with each other. I did not spend a lot of time looking at the "Transsexuals" tab, not because I wasn't curious but because many of the broadcasts came from what looked to me like a brothel in Barranquilla, Colombia.

Chaturbate first revealed its potential to be something I had not seen before on the morning I watched a twenty-seven-year-old woman named Elisa Death Naked broadcast from a house in Iceland with glass bricks, a spiral staircase, warm-looking patterned rugs, and a cozy fire crackling in the fireplace. She did not reveal her face, and instead wore, at the beginning of her striptease, a rubber horse mask with a fedora on top, along with a gray crop top, black sweatpants, and rainbow kneesocks. Her primary props were a chair painted with a replica of the Mona Lisa and a strap-on dildo. Her body had the symmetry and thinness of a catalog model, and maybe it was just the house that she was in or her high-definition camera or a general characteristic of the Icelandic people but even faceless she gleamed with the well-being that emanates wherever per-capita consumption of fish oils is high and citizens benefit from socialized health care. Her sex show, however, was strange.

"I have a pretty weird boner right now," commented one confused viewer, as Elisa changed into a Halloween mask of a ghost and began fellating her dildo. She did not interact with her audience, instead exhibiting her free-flowing sexual narrative in a manic trance. I watched her highlight reel, which showed clips from even more creative scenarios—her violently ripping apart a stuffed bear, fucking herself with a toy train, and strapping the dildo to a rocking horse and riding it. The show was a sexualized riff on the Island of Misfit Toys, plus industrial metal (the soundtrack was Rammstein). In addition to the usual Amazon Wish List (almost everyone had an Amazon Wish List for their fans to buy them things, or to bypass the website's 50 percent cut and give money directly to the performers in the form of Amazon gift cards), Elisa had links to clothes she wanted from the British online clothing store ASOS, and I clicked through them, with a vague awareness that I wanted to dress however she dressed.

In the 1990s, futurists had predicted a whole new way of having sex. "Picture yourself a couple of decades hence, getting dressed for a hot night in the virtual village," wrote the editors of the San Francisco–based *Mondo 2000* in 1992. "It would be something like a body stocking, but with all the intimate snugness of a condom. Embedded in the inner surface of the suit, using a technology that does not yet exist, is an array of intelligent effectors. These effectors are ultratiny vibrators of varying degrees of hardness, hundreds of them per square inch, that can receive and transmit a realistic sense of tactile presence in the same way the visual and audio displays transmit a realistic sense of visual and auditory presence."

This future had not come to pass. A couple of decades hence, we had some rudimentary remote-operated sex toys and no high-tech body stockings. Nobody I knew readied themselves on a Friday night for "a hot night in the virtual village." Sex online had always been divided between a passive, voyeuristic dynamic (video porn) and a more interactive one (groups of people in virtual forums verbally exciting one another in the guise of sexually avid Harry Potter characters). The latter had become a more marginal hobby. The "virtual village" most people used now, the publicly traded social networks, did not have the designated orgiastic corners that Usenet had always sustained. OkCupid and Tinder were not places to go for video sex—enabling the option would have just scared everyone away. While long-distance couples might take advantage of video chat in an erotic way, books such as *The Joy of Cybersex* and *Net Sex* were out of print. If you excluded the video assists of people in long-distance relationships, porn was the routine way of having a sexual experience via one's computer.

So I first saw Chaturbate and the many other live-sex-cam sites available online as porn. I saw them as the technological evolution of peep show booths and phone sex lines. Like those, they had a performer and they had a voyeur. The people performing did so with the intention of producing masturbatory fodder (as Chaturbate indicated in its name). I did not see an unfamiliar mode of sexual expression in My Free Cams, Live Jasmin, Cam4, or any of the many other sites that offered computerized interaction with a live human being. Seductive performance for money online was not essentially different than seductive performance in a strip club. Then I spent more time on the site.

Chaturbate was full of serendipity—I came across people like Elisa Death by chance, and sometimes I would never see them again. Some performers would schedule shows, and some had recordings of their past shows for sale, but most didn't, and you couldn't set an alarm to record a live show and watch it later. You weren't supposed to record anything, although of course people did, and the porn tubes were filled with videos ripped from Chaturbate's streams. Still, the feeling of clicking through the 18+ disclaimer into the opening matrix was the one of turning on MTV in the mid-1990s, when music videos played most of the day and kept viewers captive in the anticipation of a favorite per-former or a new discovery. Or maybe, to reach farther back in time, it recalled the early days of the Internet—the Internet of strangers rather than "friends." The earliest chat rooms on Com-puServe, back in the early 1980s, had been called "CB," in honor of the communicative free-for-all of CB radio. Here Chaturbate had revived the form, with the same initials, and the same caco-phony of ingenuity and perversion.

Some people—most people, really—did not bother to pro-vide constant masturbatory fantasy but instead would fund-raise or idly chat with their viewers in various attitudes of boredom or states of undress, with the occasional tit flash or Hitachi session to enliven the mood or fulfill the mandate of a high tipper. The best of these performers could draw in thousands of viewers by just lying around or chatting, and one felt compelled to linger and watch them the way one might put down a book to watch a house pet wander around the living room. Often, in fact, one *was* watching someone's golden retriever or tortoiseshell cat, which was usually grabbed and forced to settle peevishly in a lap. Or it was just another sex show in a kitchen, with the featured dildos lined up before a basket of lemons next to the sink like product placements in a cooking show. One woman had a cooking show, a sex and cooking show, every Friday.

Edith first appeared in a worrisome context: rolled over naked, facedown in bed after a session with her Hitachi vibrator, possibly weeping. Several of her 2,072 viewers exchanged concern: "Do you want to stop Edith?" or "What up? I clicked away and I come back and she's crying?" or "She's fucking joking" and "What happened??? She's really upset" and "I can't stand to see her sad." Then she cut off her video feed.

From watching her Chaturbate show, I learned that Edith was a nineteen-year-old college student in the Midwest who seduced her audience by dressing like an American Apparel model, revealing the depth of her existential despair, and making every one of her viewers feel as if he and only he were the person who might understand and rescue her from both her tortured soul and her vow of celibacy. This dreamy formula attracted men by the thousands, men who clamored to suggest that Edith read *Infinite Jest*, *Stranger in a Strange Land*, the research of Masters and Johnson, or the poetry of Walt Whitman, to beg her for a personal message, and to tip her when she showed them her flawless milky-white breasts, bruised knees, and untamed bush. (She had been inspired in her celebration of body hair by YouTube videos of Siouxsie and the Banshees.) She would read out loud, everything from R. D. Laing to Sam Pink. She would name-drop Michel Foucault and David Bohm. She flattered the men who watched her for their intellectual gifts and for bringing to her attention the obscure cultural artifacts they proffered in the chat bar like hipster magi. Her user name quoted a J. D. Salinger story and the first item on her Amazon Wish List was William James's *The Varieties of Religious Experience*. The second item was a long, ornately printed dress and the third item was a nun's habit. Men would discover and claim her the way that men discover and claim early electronic music from Poland or a difficult-to-reach Goan restaurant in Queens.

The second time she showed up while I was online was early one Tuesday morning. She wore a white cable-knit sweater and a 1950s-style skater skirt and stood bare-legged in a cold-looking room with white walls and tile floors. Pale winter sun filtered through one window. The room had a coffeemaker in one corner, a guitar in another, and a fabric chair of the sort made for tail-gating, with built-in beer coozies in the back. Behind her, a man dressed in a coat and scarf made coffee, ignoring Edith as she stripped down to a pale pink leotard and began fancifully danc-ing around, occasionally pulling down the leotard's straps to re-veal the rest of her body. In another corner, visible in glimpses when Edith carried her computer around the room, a woman slept under covers on an air mattress. Several sneakers and boots lay scattered around. Someone remarked that the scene looked like a flophouse out of *Breaking Bad*.

Edith had the sound off, although she would respond to compliments with a tersely typed "thank you." She breakfasted on a pint of ice cream, gazing flirtatiously at the camera. She sat down on the edge of the air mattress and lifted her skirt. Behind her, the slumbering form drew the covers in around her, and the man making coffee, or perhaps a different man (people wan-dered in and out—"there are three other people under the bed," joked one viewer), had now sat down in the beer-coozie chair and was reading a book. Their disinterest was such that it was as if

Edith were not in the room at all, as if she were a ghost. This only raised the frenzy of the chatters, who couldn't fathom how anyone could ignore such an angelic creature in their midst.

One day, Edith did a twenty-four-hour marathon on Chaturbate, which people occasionally did. She began in early afternoon, fully dressed in a blue baby-doll dress patterned with roses, smoking cigarettes in her bedroom and holding forth to an audience of more than two thousand people content just to listen to her talk. "I *will* be getting naked, absolutely, when the time comes," she said. "But if you're trying to bust a nut in ten minutes you might want to go to another room and come back." She talked about her early forays into webcamming. She had begun some six months before on the site My Free Cams, under another literary name. She was banned when she mimed hanging herself with a Hitachi Magic Wand one day when the people chatting with her started demanding illegal requests, and she switched to Chaturbate. She talked about her favorite pornos, including *Sasha Grey Takes Many Dicks*. She liked Stoya's writing but thought she was overrated—too "generic porn girl." Someone asked her if she liked James Deen. "I'm not really into male porn stars," she said.

Edith was herself contacted by a porn agent once. Initially the idea appealed to her: living in a house with other porn performers, with their own driver, hairstylists, and a swimming pool. She talked to the other girls in the house. "They all had names like Tiffany and Mercedes and they were, like, 'I get paid to bone.'" Edith mimed shooting herself in the head in exasperation. The porn agent had talked down to her, like she was a child or naive, and after some evasion of the question eventually told her the job would involve boy-girl sex. (In porn industry parlance men are boys and women are girls.) Edith was a virgin and not interested, so she did not sign up. She said she told the guy he was an "arrogant, condescending asshole" and that she "hoped his dick would fall off."

The minutes ticked by. Edith's thousands of viewers settled into their computer desk chairs and she told us more about her life. She talked about how she had graduated a year early from her high school. She took a year off after graduation, with the intention of seeking out "weird adventures." She "experimented with being homeless," living in a van for a couple of months with her two cats and integrating herself into the local homeless community. She recounted a near-death experience with elements of psychedelic mysticism. I started to wonder if Edith was some sort of Internet prophetess.

"You know, Albert Camus wrote that the only serious question in life is whether or not to kill yourself," said Edith with a solemn air of recitation. "Tom Robbins wrote that the only serious question in life is whether time has a beginning and an end. Albert Camus clearly got up on the wrong side of the bed that morning, and Tom Robbins must have forgotten to set the alarm. The real question in life is who knows how to make love stay. Answer me that, and I will tell you not to kill yourself. Answer me that, and I will ease your mind from the beginning to the end of time."

What the fuck was I watching? I closed my laptop and went out to dinner.

I looked in at midnight and the camera was trained on an empty bed. Even empty, her room held the number-three spot on the website. Twelve hours later, I looked again. For more than 1,700 viewers she sat on the floor naked next to a pair of ballet slippers with an unlit cigarette in her hand. Some of her chatters wanted more sex. Most of them didn't care. "She can do whatever she wants," wrote one. "I'm lucky to be here and having fun with the best lady in the universe."

During the final minutes of her marathon, some of the chatters indicated they had stayed up all night with her, but she did not end with an extravagant sexual act. Instead she had put on another of her endless collection of cute floral dresses and sat against the wall next to a pile of books. She was pale, with circles under her eyes. In the last five minutes she honored her highest tippers by listing them by name. Who were these men? Earlier, I had clicked over to the webcam of one high tipper, who had also served as her moderator. He had posted his location as Germany and hidden his face. All that was visible, in standard desk-light illumination, was the bottom of an unshaven chin, the ends of his long curly hair, his shirtless torso, and a black denim jacket with "Trans-Siberian Orchestra" embroidered in white over the breast pocket.

When the final seconds of her marathon expired, Edith sat up. "Did I make it?" she asked. "It happened?" A chorus of chatters affirmed she had made it. She threw her hands into the air and shrieked. Then she leaned forward, as if to embrace her laptop, and severed the video feed. The time was 2:30 p.m.

I called Edith, but she didn't want her parents to find out about her activities. She declined to be interviewed after the first phone call and said she was going to quit Chaturbate. On the phone, she had affirmed that she was not sexually active in real life, although she had gone out with boyfriends in the past and had once performed with her female roommate on Chaturbate. She said she was otherwise celibate, and had considered that she might be "Internet sexual."

Edith said she had made $1,500 during the twenty-four-hour marathon, but that she spent a lot of her earnings tipping other cam girls. One of her favorites, a cammer named Doxie, had bought her the requested copy of William James. I watched Doxie's webcam once. She had suspended herself by the arms from the ceiling on a hook made of ice, blindfolded herself, and wired up some kind of sex machine that vibrated every time someone tipped her. Until the ice melted, she was trapped at the mercy of the vibrating machine. For so much effort she only had about three hundred people watching her. Then I watched an archived video of her masturbating on a ski lift. She was thirty-three, on the older side for Chaturbate, where most of the performers were in their twenties, and her bio said she was living at home caring for her mother, who had cancer. Caring for an ailing relative was a situation I encountered many times while interviewing people about live webcams. Doxie's Amazon Wish List consisted largely of blacksmithing supplies.

Was Doxie also "Internet sexual"? Was Edith? Were others? One evening, a few days after I watched her spank herself twenty-four times with a paddle at midnight on her twenty-fourth birthday, I Skyped with a woman who performed under the name Karastë (the name, which means "dearest" in Swedish, is pronounced *sha-rist-ah*). As she performed, Karastë had gently chastised viewers who tried to tell her what to do. "That's not how this room works," she said. "No requests, no coaching, no directing. I move in my own time, right? Because consent is key." Her fans did not mind. "I have no idea how anybody genetically scored the most outstanding body on earth," wrote one.

Karastë had long red hair and large breasts and the patient demeanor of a kindergarten teacher. She first went on Chaturbate in December 2013, after hearing about it from a friend. At the time, she said, she was experiencing what she called a "sexual lull," a description she quickly amended: "That's not a good word, because it was from the inception of my sexuality—like from the very start to up until the Chaturbate point—that it was in a lull."

She was raised in the south as a Southern Baptist and lived in the Southeastern city where she grew up. During two long-term relationships that had been her introduction to sex, she had disliked having sex and felt deeply insecure about her body. "I hated sex and I was also really blurry on the rules of consent, because that was not taught to me either," she said. "In retrospect there were a lot of things that happened that should have never happened, because of that lack of education." Without the Internet, she said, "I would have been reading *Good Housekeeping* and working out how to fake an orgasm better."

When she saw Chaturbate, she thought she might use it as a tool to overcome the psychological barriers she had about sex. She also thought she could perform on it and remain secret, but a former high school classmate saw her and told all their friends. "He's a bit of a men's rights activist," she explained. (Karastë's shows often became discussions about feminism, or just about why an unsolicited dick pic might make a woman unhappy. They revealed that another positive aspect of Chaturbate was to serve as a safe space for men and women to have frank discussions about sexuality, and one with a better gender balance than the population on, say, a pickup artist subreddit.)

She called Chaturbate an "introvert's paradise." I asked her how it was that broadcasting her image to thousands of people over the Internet could appeal to an introvert.

"I have complete control over the situation," she said. "I don't have to worry about it escalating physically. I can turn it off whenever I want. I can turn these words on the screen off whenever I want. I can kick people out. I make my own rules, nobody's telling me what to do. Not that I'm necessarily a control freak, but I'd never had that sexually. I'd never been in control of a sexual encounter until this, and I think it was something that I definitely needed."

I met Wendy Bird through Stoner Boner, and it was through Wendy that I came to understand a whole side of Chaturbate that I had not previously contemplated, that there were women—and of course there were—who went on the site not to receive a flood of compliments from perverts but to perv themselves, to objectify and commune with the legion young men who sat in the glow of a thousand desk lamps in search of a woman, any woman, who might miraculously grace them with some individual sexual attention.

Stoner Boner was a twenty-one-year-old gay man in Alabama, who, when I first talked to him in early 2014, had just reached his first anniversary on Chaturbate. He had joined the site in 2013 as a joke; two years later he had more than 25,000 followers. Stoner felt that broadcasting sex on a live webcam would become like go-go dancing was in the 1960s, a youthful embarrassment for future offspring to make fun of. "This is going to be the thing with our generation," he said. "I think cam modeling, or having a porn blog, that's going to be the thing we did."

Chaturbate's performers might have been a young sexual vanguard but its viewers were frequently of a different generation. One of Stoner Boner's followers, who also served as a moderator on his website, was Wendy Bird. Wendy was a forty-four-year-old woman in Iowa. She was single, an artist. She had recently left the liberal college town where she had been living and returned to the small town she grew up in to care for her ailing father. Wendy had never been that interested in computers, but at some point she discovered she liked to guide people through their masturbatory fantasies. One day she was doing one such voice-only session with a man when he said he was going to simulcast the event through his webcam to Chaturbate. Wendy went to the site. "I had never done anything like that and I never thought I would," she said. "I was even late to get a cell phone."

First she just watched, mostly men. Then one day she turned on her camera, trained it on a bookshelf, and began speaking over it. Now, after entering what she called a "hermit phase" of her life, she had discovered "mass intimacy." People began coming into her chat room and encouraging her. Soon she turned the camera on her mouth and began doing shows that way. Chaturbate banned her for possibly being underage, "which was kind of funny." She went through the steps to get her age verified, sending a photo of herself holding her ID next to her face, scanning in a copy of her driver's license. Finally she put her face on camera and began performing under the name Khaleesi_Heart_ (a reference to *Game of Thrones*). She made friends, "lifelong close friendships," through Chaturbate, some of whom she had met in person, though not for sex. One helped her move; another came and visited when he was having some trouble at home.

One night, Wendy Bird, Stoner Boner, and I engaged with what Wendy called "multiperving." We audio-Skyped with one another while sifting through videos online. Wendy showed me how to set up my profile to broadcast, and then turn it password-only so I wouldn't show up on the main site. Then she asked me what I liked. What I *liked*? We scrolled through the matrix of men. They looked so young. "Objectify them," Wendy encouraged me.

From the beginning of her experience, Wendy had bypassed what she called the "zombie hot girls" that populated the site's main page. She would go for the men, but not even the most popular men, instead clicking through to the second or third pages for the real amateurs, the forest of men in desk chairs that I had studiously avoided. It turned out they waited there for a reason. "A lot of the hetero guys are doing it so that they will find someone who will cam-to-cam with them," she explained, adding that here, where hopes resided in the chance of an electronic encounter between two people, tokens mattered much less. If, on its landing page, Chaturbate was thousands of men watching a few women, a couple of pages in, the numbers changed to one or two people using Chaturbate to interact privately with another person. Wendy used Chaturbate not merely for voyeurism, but to arrange virtual casual encounters. She had her pick of possibilities, finding enough willing men to have electronic intimacy at any hour of the day. "Once they know you're game, they're like '*please*,'" she explained, adding that her first experience of the breadth of such desire, the number of men lusting for interaction, had felt intoxicating. She encouraged me to find a guy I thought looked nice and she would show me how it worked.

I wrote a message to a guy lying in bed wearing nothing but a pair of Ray-Bans. From her computer, Wendy clicked on his page and wrote, "Emily is new, we are chatting off CB and I'm teaching her the ropes right now." Wendy predicted that the minute "Mark Smith" knew we were women, he would want us to broadcast to him. She was right: he wasted no time. "One of you should go online," he typed in reply. So I turned on my camera, made it password-accessible, and gave him the password. I sat there in my bedroom, fully clothed, insisting nervously that I was just testing things out. He kept encouraging me to join him in nudity. I refused and apologized. Wendy encouraged me not to apologize—I could remain fully clothed if I wanted to. I was embarrassed to have Wendy and Stoner Boner on the line, but they knew they had taught me to crack a code; they had taught me how to engineer a private and anonymous online sexual encounter, and they giggled wickedly at my embarrassment.

"There's this freedom, in that you don't actually have to meet any of these people and they don't actually know you," Wendy explained. "You can be whoever you want to be. You can show them any part of yourself that you want. You can be totally open and bare and share everything without having to worry about people rejecting you or you can totally make up a new self and be someone different."

I'd recently read an essay in a book called *Times Square Red, Times Square Blue* by the science fiction writer Samuel R. Delany, a gay African-American man who had spent years in the 1970s and 1980s frequenting the porno movie theaters in Times Square, where he had hundreds of casual and anonymous sexual encounters with other men. He wrote that it was a shame that women suffered risks in the pursuit of similar experiences, but that also "What waits is for enough women to consider such venues as a locus of possible pleasure."

He went on to describe the benefits of his vast experience in casual sex. The movie theaters had served as laboratories in which he had learned to discern the nuances and spectrum of his sexual desire, where sexual experimentation happened entirely outside narratives of love or emotional entanglement. His observations about sexual attraction consistently disproved conventional notions of beauty and ugliness. (He discovered, among other proclivities, that he had a thing for burly Irish-American men, including two who had harelips.) Describing the importance of the anonymous sexual encounter, he wrote:

> We do a little better when we sexualize our own manner of having sex—learn to find our own way of having sex sexy. Call it a healthy narcissism, if you like. This alone allows us to relax with our own sexuality. Paradoxically, this also allows us to vary it and accommodate it, as far as we wish, to other people. I don't see how this can be accomplished without a statistically

significant variety of partners and a fair amount of communication with them, at that, about what their sexual reactions to
us are. (However supportive, the response of a single partner
just cannot do that. This is a quintessentially *social* process, in-
volving a social response.)

For women, the pursuit of wide-ranging sexual experience
had always come with disproportionate risks and stigma. But
online, in the context of what Wendy called "mass intimacy," some
of the women I spoke with were undertaking Delany's endeavor
with the risk of pregnancy, violence, and sexually transmitted infection minimized through the medium of encounter. Chaturbate
and its ilk—everything from My Free Cams to the Gone Wild
amateur porn thread on Reddit—could be the equivalent of the
darkened porno theater of the twenty-first century, but places
more welcoming to women, where women could go to consider
their desires, where they could learn what attracted others to
them, and discern and name what they found attractive.

Traffic estimates indicated that visitors to Chaturbate were
overwhelmingly more male than female. The sexual perfor-
mances that I found most intriguing were usually happening in
the corners of the website, and felt contrary to Chaturbate's expectation and design. If there was ever going to be a site specifically promoting anonymous sexual exploration for women, a
place for the encounters in numbers that Delany found so important to his self-knowledge, Chaturbate would not be it. I pictured spaces on the Internet free of sidebars advertising lonely
MILFs where women went for digital manhandling by handsome strangers using advanced teledildonic technology. The worry
that the encounter would be recorded or that its data would be
hacked punctured the serenity of the dream.

The performers of Chaturbate had economic as well as sexual motivation. In talking to people who earned money on the site, a pattern emerged, of a society where wages were so low that they were no longer worth striving for, where ambitious young people could not advance their education without going into debt, and where the misfortune of illness resulted in financial catastrophe. For the people in phases of their lives where they had to serve as caretaker to an ill partner or relative, the sex work offered flexibility, even if their earnings were often unpredictable or paltry. Other people I interviewed, including Karastë and a woman from upstate New York who went by the user name of JingleTits, were in their early twenties and saw themselves in an intermediary phase between high school and a hoped-for future in college. They had concrete career ambitions but their families were unable to assist them with the cost of higher education. Those young people who had gotten a college education found themselves questioning the worth of their degrees, and saw masturbating on camera for money as being less humiliating and offering more opportunities for meaningful and creative endeavor than the jobs they saw as available to them. One such couple was Max and Harper.

Max and Harper met on OkCupid in spring of 2011. Harper was twenty years old and a student of English literature at a college in Washington State, out east for the summer to work as a nanny in New Jersey. Max was twenty-six, moonlighted as an improv comic, worked at a restaurant in Tribeca, and slept on a love seat in a shared apartment in Harlem. Their first date began in Times Square and ended the next morning at the Port Authority, where Harper caught the bus back to Jersey. Six months later Max moved to Washington to be with her.

Out west, Max had trouble finding a job he liked. He was hired at Starbucks but quit out of boredom during latte training. In November 2012, to pick up some cash, the young couple began sex camming on the website Live Jasmin. It was fun, but Live Jasmin had a lot of rules. A cammer could not eat, drink, or wear logos while the camera recorded. Until someone paid to enter into a private chat, the models just sat on their beds fully clothed, hustling like prostitutes in the windows of Amsterdam's red light district. "It was a lot of waiting around, trying to trick people into doing a show with you, just selling it hard," said Harper. It still felt like a job, in other words, but a job that Harper liked more than her actual job, which consisted of "hanging pants on hangers and making small talk with people I don't like."

Live Jasmin also had rules to make its performers act like "cam models," with the obsequious pliancy and sweet demeanor that characterize the collective adulation of the male ego on most sex sites. For Max and Harper, the whole point of sex camming was to avoid customer service. What they envisioned making together instead would be like the low-budget amateur variety shows that used to be found on the old cable-access channels; "*Wayne's World* with tits," as Max described it. At other times they referred to it as "digital street performance." In the summer of 2013, Max found Chaturbate.

On Chaturbate, from a single account, they could perform alone or together or have a threesome. They could make Max conduct an endurance test where Harper dipped his penis in ice water and counted to thirty. She could sit in a Starbucks and silently reveal her breasts to the camera. They could have puppet shows, and threesomes, and a food fight. Harper could give Max a henna tattoo of a rooster with a giant erection. They could hang their Christmas lights on the wall behind them to spell out FUCK. They could reward high tippers by recording video of themselves stripped naked and running down the street yelling, "I AM THE KING/QUEEN OF SCOTLAND." Within two months of joining they amassed more than 20,000 followers (eventually they reached more than 81,000). Some days were slow, but on others their audiences reached more than 7,000 people.

Through the money they started earning, they also began to envision another kind of freedom. The idea to buy a van came to Max on a mushroom trip, one summer in 2013 as the sun set over a field in Washington State. He hallucinated a conversation with an entity that Max, an atheist, could only call God.

A few weeks later, Harper and Max used their combined $1,000 in savings to purchase a 1994 Ford Aerostar for $900. They decided to shed their material belongings and Chaturbate their way across the country. They called their show "Fucking in Fifty," and they even recorded a peppy theme song ("We're gonna hit the road / we're gonna help you cum . . .")

On the road, they learned how to survive with less than ten dollars in their bank account. They learned how to work the food banks and tap into Wi-Fi networks and to live on the fringes of a country bloated with caloric and technological excess. Their appearances changed: from a mop-headed, clean shaven young man in cargo shorts and Vibram barefoot running shoes, Max went full-on Allen Ginsberg in appearance. His beard grew black and thick, his hair long; he began wearing his black plastic glasses more often than not. Harper went from being a blue-eyed, strawberry-blond sorority girl with a layered haircut and baggy jeans to having pierced nipples and long, wavy hair.

When Max and Harper got frustrated with their off-the-grid life, they usually evoked the specter of OfficeMax. Or, after a particularly enthusiastic session of sex on camera, they would high-five, and one would ask the other, "Want to quit and go work at OfficeMax?" The joke was about all that was wrong in the world, to Harper and Max: big-box stores in concrete lots, the drudgery of the dead-end hourly wage, beige filing cabinets, obedience, the myth that hard work for a multinational corporation would be rewarded in any significant way.

They drove around the country. An investor gave them $4,000 to build their website. They decided to pass the winter in Mexico. Then all of their equipment and laptops were stolen. Their investor was arrested for trafficking drugs and arms on Silk Road.

A video lingers on PornHub of Max and Harper having sex on a rainy afternoon in Puerto Vallarta. Through the curtained windows of what looks like a cheap hotel room, Mexico is a place of barking dogs and customized car horns. For the first time, Max and Harper showed signs of regret.

"The date is February 18, 2014," they wrote on their blog. "Harper and Max are stuck in Mexico with 200 dollars remaining." They renounced "Fucking in Fifty." "I sought to build myself a pleasant future and once again I seem to have only succeeded in building myself a cage," wrote Max.

Their fans bailed them out, and they returned to the United States. They landed in Idaho, renting a room from a friend they made on FetLife, the social network for people who are into kinky sex. In the fall of 2014, Max and Harper helped their friend start a custom-made spanking paddle business to pay off some of the vast medical debts he incurred during the treatment of his eleven-year-old daughter's leukemia. They experimented with fire play.

Chaturbate, meanwhile, changed its rules. Public sex, a mainstay for Harper and Max, who broadcast from hay fields and rest stops, from McDonald's, Starbucks, Walmarts, and even a McDonald's inside a Walmart—was no longer allowed. Tired of the hustle of Chaturbate, of the unpredictability of tipping, they found a new income stream, a website called Clips 4 Sale that catered to obscure sexual fetishes. Harper and Max began to spend their days recording clips appealing to people with fetishes about women wearing aprons or ripping off their clothes. Harper climbed the charts and for a time became the number one belcher on the site. They made foot-fetish videos with Vibram barefoot running sneakers. They lived happily on an income that ranged from $400 to $2,000 a month. The last time I spoke with them, their plan was to buy a bus and eventually a piece of land. They called it "the quest."

As Max and Harper went deeper into their online sexual exploration, they learned that sex was no longer a thing either of them could define. "I know intercourse is definable as a thing but I don't, like, *believe* in 'sex,'" said Max. "I don't think I could point to it, I couldn't tell you what it is, because for some people, completely clothed just-pulling-at-your-nostrils-at-a-camera is sex, it's a massive turn-on."

Some people might have looked at Max and Harper, or anybody on Chaturbate, and disagreed. They might think of clean sheets, a well-made bed, a clearly defined "partner," and a closed door and think that they know exactly what sex is—loving, maybe; monogamous, probably; dignified by its secrecy; more authentic for not being shared; sacred because it's not mediated through a cell phone. Such a view was starting to feel both rarified and unambitious.

POLYAMORY

For generations, young people had flocked to San Francisco for the promise of a queer community, or a rave scene, or Beatnik literature, or to adorn one another with flowers in the sunlit haze of Golden Gate Park. By 2012 the young people who came to San Francisco were neither dropouts nor misfits nor the victims of prejudice. They were children who had grown up eating sugar-free cereal, swaddled in Polar Fleece jackets made from recycled plastic bottles. They had studied abroad in West Africa and volunteered in high school at local soup kitchens. They knew their favorite kinds of sashimi, and were friends with their parents. They expressed their emotions in the language of talk therapy. Unlike their parents, they commuted to the suburbs, and lived in the cities. As they arrived, the cities they arrived in changed in their image, reshaped to receive the new generation's disposable income.

San Francisco was one such city, but Denver, Boston, Portland,

Austin, and Brooklyn's Williamsburg all bore traces of the same cultural shift. It was as if the cities where the privileged youth flocked evolved in neatly parallel trajectories, the culmination of which were prancing shih tzus, five-dollar toast, and healthy fast-food restaurants with names like Zeal, Thrive, and Lyfe. The young people went to coffee shops where the production of espresso was ritualized to resemble a historic reenactment of the hardships of nineteenth-century pioneer life. Nobody smoked cigarettes. They honed their bodies with the aim of either perfect homeostasis or eternal life. They knew about the benefits of the iodine in wakame and the selenium in Brazil nuts. They ate red meat only once a month, to time their consumption of iron with the end of their menstrual cycles.

The young people dressed casually. They reverted on weekends to workout clothes, when they went hiking with their dogs. They enjoyed wholesome fun, and it was not surprising to see in San Francisco groups of young men carrying around boxes of board games, going to play Settlers of Catan and drink beer, but beer that had been flavored according to the season, beer bottles that carried quaint illustrations on their labels. They started companies whose names referenced fantasy fiction. They were adults, but they could seem like children, because they were so positive, because they liked to play, because they were marketed to with bright colors, clean, day-lit spaces, and nutritious snacks, and because their success was in part attributed to the fact that they had arrived in early adulthood and apparently had never broken any rules. Their sex lives were impossible to fathom, because they seemed never to have lived in darkness. They had grown up observing foreign wars, economic inequality, and ecological catastrophe, crises that they earnestly discussed on their digital feeds but avoided internalizing as despair.

I'm not saying Elizabeth was all of these things but she described herself as an optimist. Elizabeth had a membership at a rock-climbing gym; she meditated; when practicing yoga she could do an inversion without the support of a wall. She organized activities: hot-air balloon rides, weekend trips to Sea Ranch. She worked long, punishing hours, but had the energy and the vacation days to stay up all night on weekends, go on cycling excursions, or attend silent contemplative retreats.

A friend of mine had met her at a circus arts class. My friend had suggested I might want to speak with her but also tried to explain: "The thing about all the polyamorists I know . . ." my friend started to say, as we sat in a karaoke piano bar in Oakland drinking greyhounds. It felt good to leave San Francisco, which was like visiting a planet made of pastel marzipan, for Oakland, which had garishly lit gas stations, community-police conflict, and prominent fast-food establishments. With my phone I took a picture of a business card taped to the wall that read: GINA: READER AND ADVISOR, SPECIALIZING IN ALL MATTERS IN LIFE. "The thing about polyamorists," my friend continued, "is that they are all so *self-confident*."

Elizabeth had moved to San Francisco after college. Her boyfriend from college moved to a mid-size city in the south to go to medical school. No matter how much she loved him, or how much her mother, an infertility specialist, urged her to have children as a young woman, she was not yet ready to marry and start a family. She had a job offer as a consultant at an economics firm. So, in 2010, when she was twenty-two, she moved west, he went south, and they broke up.

Elizabeth had never before lived in a city. She knew the suburbs in Virginia where she had grown up, and the small New England town where she had attended college. She arrived in San Francisco and made friends, some of them by Internet dating. She met Wes one night in late 2010, when he accompanied one of her co-workers to a board game party at her house. He flirted with her. They played a spatial reasoning game called Blokus. Elizabeth won.

For their first date, they attended "Nerd Night" at a local bar. They watched a lecture about the future of teledildonics. They ended their date with a walk to the edge of Dolores Park, where the city spread out below, blinking on and off. On the walk home, they kissed on a street corner. Then Wes, with the transparency he thought of as mature and fair, gave a speech of preemptive relationship indemnity. He was still getting over his last girl-friend, he said. He did not want to be in a relationship. Elizabeth tried not to roll her eyes—it was the first date! They said good night and parted ways.

Wes had grown up in San Francisco, studied computer science at Harvard, and returned west after graduation to work at Google. Like thousands of others, he rode the unmarked white bus each day to Google's office park in Mountain View, where he grazed from multiethnic food stations in the cafeterias and stared at computers. Somewhere along the upward incline of his preco-cious youth he had skipped a grade and was still only twenty-one, tall and handsome in a preppy J. Crew catalog kind of way.

Wes's previous serious relationship, the one before he met Elizabeth, had ended his senior year of college. At the time he met Elizabeth, the discovery of how much he liked casual sex was therefore still new to him, less than a year old. As a former shy person, his romantic eligibility was also a novel phenome-non. Women who once would have ignored him now paid atten-tion to him. When he smiled at them they smiled back. Sex with them taught him about what he liked and what they liked and about the great diversity of women's sexual interests. Now, back in San Francisco, he could click through OkCupid with the reas-surance that he had grown away from whatever he had once been: a studious child who had close friends but whose friends consisted of other boys who did math problems and read books. Casual sex allowed him to inhabit his newfound ease in the world. This was what he meant when he told Elizabeth that he was not interested in a relationship.

Still, Elizabeth and Wes lived only three blocks away from each other. They began meeting once a week for drinks, dates, and sleeping over, always with a show of nonchalance. Given the choice, Elizabeth would have wanted a more serious commitment. She was only twenty-three but she had one reaction to Wes's lack of interest in their relationship: he was acting like a baby. Girls, she felt, "age in dog years." Fine, she decided. She would also continue to date. She would also see other people.

A few weeks later, through a friend, she met Brian, a graduate of Stanford who also worked in tech. Soon Elizabeth had two nonboyfriends. Neither relationship had the expectation of exclusivity, or any defined path into the future. She kept the two relationships separate and never saw the men together. They balanced each other, with one providing security against the possible failure of the other. The balance kept her calm.

The two relationships gave her two different social scenes, sentimental roles, and ways of being. With Brian, she had an intense sexual connection. She shared with him her interests in yoga and meditation. He was a few years older, and already had lots of friends in the city. He had gone to Burning Man for years running and introduced her to the subculture of Burners in town, who had brought back from the playa certain principles of fast intimacy, do-it-yourself maker culture, and mind expansion.

With these new friends, Elizabeth tried drugs for the first time. She had not taken drugs before because she obeyed rules and thought that people who did drugs did not succeed in life. In college, the people Elizabeth had known who took psilocybin mushrooms, LSD, and MDMA had done so, it seemed to her, to escape thinking about their problems, or simply to stay up all night. Brian's friends did their exploration with a different intention: not to temporarily forget their reality but to better understand it. They took MDMA and psychedelics to form deeper connections with their friends. They stayed up all night, too. Doing drugs had not affected their success in life. Few groups of young people in the history of the United States had ever been so successful.

Elizabeth did not love Brian. But Wes . . . Wes was also new to the city. He had graduated from college the same year. They shared a worldview. Friends noted their synchronized mechanization, two people rarely disrupted by uncontrolled emotion, as atomically stable as the noble gases. With Brian, Elizabeth was the innocent pilgrim. With Wes she got to be the explorer and guide. One day in May 2011, six months after meeting each other, Elizabeth introduced Wes to psilocybin mushrooms. They went to Golden Gate Park, where the eucalyptus glades are redolent with the collective memory of half-envisioned entities and fragmented glimpses into other dimensions. Elizabeth has a photo from that day of Wes, supine on a bed of brown pine needles and twigs. His gaze is upward, his sunglasses reflect tree branches and sky. He lies in a gray coat and blue T-shirt with one hand half-raised above him, the other in his pocket, a Moleskine notebook by his side still in its plastic wrapper. The mushroom trip shifted their relationship. They still did not use the word *love*, but they now acknowledged what they referred to as "emotional involvement."

They avoided the words *boyfriend* and *girlfriend*. When they went for dinner with Wes's family, Elizabeth was presented as a friend. Spring passed into summer—longer days, more fog, repetitious quotation of Mark Twain to visitors who didn't bring a wool parka for the cold July nights, leathery-tan nudists twinkling at passersby in the Castro, stone fruit season at Bi-Rite. Somewhere down in Palo Alto Steve Jobs was on his deathbed, the white aura of the battery light pulsing ever more faint. San Francisco, 2011: the Summer of Emotional Involvement.

That August, Elizabeth went to Burning Man with Brian and took LSD for the first time. When she emerged from her trip she felt she had changed—not by embracing a new enthusiasm for hippie metaphysics (the scripts she had been raised with about ambition and career remained intact, and one starts to wonder what exactly the hippies claimed to have seen—enlightenment, a new world order, God . . .). Her conviction upon resurfacing was only that some vital part of human nature could reach satisfaction only in the context of a primal carnival, desert-based or otherwise, that had elements of uninhibited intoxication, long nights fading into sunrises, trance-inducing music, leather, headdresses. Some countries had ritualized bacchanal into the annual calendar. America had not, and could not see revels without anticipation of atonement, without smug speculation about consequences. Humans were supposed to be silly from time to time, was what Elizabeth now suspected—also that the anticipated punishment for having too much fun would not arrive like an answer to a question. Punishment might, in fact, never arrive at all.

On the final Saturday of the festival, when the Burning Man was set on fire and tens of thousands of people converged in the expanse of the desert to dance, Elizabeth met a man. He was an engineer, so probably smart. He smelled bad but it was Burning Man. She was on MDMA, feeling as certain as a plumb line, as constant as neon. The dust was velveteen, the sky concave and luminous, the music circadian. She fell in and out of love on the same roll, but they had sex, and she confirmed a second fundamental principle of the way she wanted to be in the world, something she had felt since the first time she took MDMA. She would not ignore suffering, because suffering was real, but she had no reason not to be happy. Two things to remember from then forward: happiness as a guiding principle, happiness above all, and what Simone de Beauvoir once called "the fête"—"an impassioned apotheosis of the present in the face of anxiety concerning the future."

Back in San Francisco, Elizabeth did not yet attach her newfound dedication to a life of heightened experience with a set of particular plans. It was more like setting aside a vacant room that would be furnished when she had more time or money. For now, her ideas of adult life were unchanged: work as hard as possible; someday get married and have kids. Left to think about it long enough, she could still work herself into indignation that Wes would not "grow up" and fully commit to her. That fall, he went to London for two weeks for work. In his absence Elizabeth vowed to break up with him. She changed her mind before he boarded at Heathrow for the return flight. She had her work to focus on, especially once she, too, was hired at Google. Now they took the bus to Mountain View and ate in the cafeteria together.

Elizabeth did not describe what she was doing—having sex with two men on a regular basis over an extended period of time, with the occasional extrarelationship dalliance besides—as polyamory. *Polyamory* was a neologism one absorbed in San Francisco just by breathing the air, but it was also a key term in an extended regional palaver that prompted people from other parts of the country to roll their eyes, not so much at the rejection of monogamy but rather at the earnestness and jargon with which it was discussed.

The word was still new. When the *Oxford English Dictionary* had added *polyamory* in 2006, it cited as first usage a 1992 Internet post suggesting the creation of an alt.poly-amory Usenet newsgroup. Other sources traced the word to a woman named

Morning Glory Ravenheart-Zell, who first used the adjective *poly-amorous* in a magazine article in 1990 about the logistics of her open marriage.

According to *The Encyclopedia of Witchcraft, Witches and Wicca*, Ravenheart-Zell, née Diana Moore, was born in 1948 in Long Beach, California. She changed her name to Morning Glory at the age of nineteen because she felt she could not worship the goddess Diana, whose disciples in ancient Rome had practiced chastity. She met her first husband while hitchhiking to a commune in Eugene, Oregon, in 1969; she left him for her second husband, Oberon Zell-Ravenheart (né Timothy Zell), in 1973. They fell in love at Gnosticon, an annual meeting of neo-pagans.

From the beginning of their forty-year marriage, the Ravenheart-Zells continued having relationships with other people, including the formation of a triad that lasted a decade. It was at the behest of one of her husband's partners that Morning Glory published an explanatory article called "A Bouquet of Lovers" in *Green Egg*, the magazine of the neo-pagan Church of All Worlds. Earlier words that attempted to describe what the Ravenheart-Zells called "the idea of having multiple simultaneous sexual/loving relationships without necessarily marrying everyone," terms ventured in early Internet forums and in the pages of the free-love magazine *Loving More*, included *polyfidelity, omnigamy, panfidelity*, and *nonmonogamy*. Instead of using either the Greek or the Latin translations for "loving many," which would have resulted in "polyphilia" (sounds like a pathology) or "multiamory" (like a plug adaptor), Ravenheart-Zell, intrepid philologist, combined the two: poly-amory. She also wrote about the rules her extended sexual network had developed to manage their relationships. One rule was the "Condom Cadre," an agreement among five people to use condoms with everyone outside their circle.

Morning Glory Ravenheart-Zell died of cancer in May 2014, long after the word she coined had outgrown its New Age roots. From free spirits who discussed the existence of unicorns the word had passed quickly into the small Internet newsgroup communities of the early 1990s and out into wider culture. Still, by 1997, the year that guides such as *The Ethical Slut* by Dossie Easton and Janet Hardy, and Deborah Anapol's *Polyamory*, were published, the notion mainly remained confined to the cities of Northern California where the hippies had resisted mass extinction. Dan Savage, the widely syndicated newspaper sex columnist whose open-minded advice could serve as a barometer of the concerns of sexually active, freethinking young professionals in America's major cities, had only a single mention of "polyamory" in a collection of his columns published in 1998, and that was an explanatory definition—an introduction of the term for a person writing in with questions about a love triangle. Savage wrote that he preferred the term *polyfidelity*.

By the time Elizabeth went to Burning Man for the first time in 2011, the festival included many teach-ins and lectures on managing polyamorous relationships, but the word had accrued cultural connotations for her, of swinging married people or creepy old men who hit on young women. It seemed to her that the word had more to do with how a certain kind of person liked to present herself to the world, as maverick or on the fringe, than it did with any practicable methodology of managing relationships. Although like most people her age she had friends whose dyadic partnerships allowed for sex with other people, those friends tended to use the term "open relationship," which was somehow less infused with the stigma of intentional weirdness, and did not amount to a proclamation of sexual identity.

Still, whatever accidental arrangement she had created, and

despite her own enjoyment of her freedoms, by the end of that year the lack of sexual boundaries was causing her no small amount of anxiety. Wes's crushes from high school were resurfacing. Women on OkCupid were probably sending him winky emoticons by the dozens. To allay her growing insecurity, she turned to self-help, and read *The Ethical Slut*.

The Ethical Slut, "A Practical Guide to Polyamory, Open Relationships & Other Adventures," is a useful but at times overly chirpy book. Its baby boomer co-authors, Janet Hardy and Dossie Easton, trace their inquiry into free love to the utopianism of the 1960s. They begin by questioning the universally desirable outcome of a monogamous marriage, an institution they see as neither "normal" nor "natural." The ideal of monogamy, they write, pertained to obsolete agrarian cultures. It now coasts on tradition, especially because people seeking to pursue a sexual life beyond the ideal of marriage face a vacuum of prescribed behaviors and ethics: "We have no culturally approved scripts for open sexual lifestyles," they write. "We need to write our own." They proceed with taxonomies of possible sexual identities and strategies for maintaining health, stability, and "unlearning jealousy." They revive the word *slut* as a "reclamation," to mean "a person of any gender who celebrates sexuality according to the radical proposition that sex is nice and pleasure is good for you."

Co-written by a psychotherapist and a writer, the book presupposes a lot more unembarrassed discussion than many people may feel capable of having with their sexual partners. Happily proclaiming oneself a "slut" is itself a difficult proposition: the word carries the memory of its negative, gendered history, no matter how flippantly it is repurposed. It seems especially unsympathetic to those people pursuing an alternative sexual ethics out of resignation rather than enthusiasm. (I did not, for example, think of being single as my choice to "be in a relationship with myself.") Still, since its first publication the book has sold more than 160,000 copies.

Practicing polyamorists describe a phase they call "joining the book club." Elizabeth followed *The Ethical Slut* with the evolutionary biology bestseller *Sex at Dawn*, by Christopher Ryan and Cacilda Jetha, who argue that humans have evolved to enjoy sex with multiple partners as part of our inexorable primate destiny. Then she read Tristan Taormino's *Living Open*, another guide to managing sex with multiple partners.

Joining the book club gave Elizabeth permission to consider that not everybody had to live the vision of adulthood that she had expected to live growing up. The monogamous couple, an institution she had always thought of as a default outcome, suddenly took on the appearance of a deliberate choice. Once she saw monogamy as a choice, and not a given, it began to take on the cast of an unreasonable expectation, best suited to people who disliked experimentation—people not like her.

Elizabeth grew up surrounded by Southern Baptists in Virginia. Her father was a Korean immigrant and her mother was Jewish, the religion in which she was raised. As a child, she had a powerful curiosity about sex. She first tried masturbating in the second grade, after hearing somebody talking about it on television. She had thought of what she did as bad and did not discuss her experiments with any of her friends. By middle school she had decided to educate herself further by watching Internet porn. It was partially curiosity and partially because it turned her on, but porn also became a way to gauge the extent to which she was attracted to women as well as men. When Elizabeth was in middle school, her dad opened her laptop one day to a video of a rowdy lesbian caper. He deleted the files, closed the computer, and left the room. They never discussed the matter.

Elizabeth had sex for the first time at fourteen, while visiting Miami for a swim meet. Her partner was sixteen, and also a virgin, or at least he claimed to be one. They have stayed friends on Facebook.

She started her first serious sexual relationship at the age of fifteen and started taking the birth control pill. She thinks of herself as lucky: for never having had many negative feelings about sex, for being comfortable with her sexuality, and for never having been the victim of sexual violence. At college she had sex with three people her freshman year, and made out with several more. While nobody judged her, the way the other students discussed sex in college caused her to police herself. She would watch rumors spread about specific men or women and their sexual histories. She saw the power such rumors could have. Although she found the gossip backward, she found it easier and more convenient to comply with a sexually conservative façade. Her sophomore year, she saw one man consistently.

More worrisome to her was the prospect of how her sexual behavior could be used against her as she tried to cultivate a professional reputation. In college, she began working as a teaching assistant to an economics professor, and it became very important to her that her students did not know if she had hooked up with their friends. As she grew older, the stakes seemed only to be higher. She suspected that talking at work about her multiple lovers could sabotage her career. She was confronting, if not a double standard along gendered lines, at least a sort of foundational hypocrisy: where ambition, curiosity, and a willingness to take risks in one's professional life was kept separate from the mirage of propriety that governed one's personal life. Monogamy was assimilated into notions of leadership and competence; other sexual choices came with loss of authority. The fear of falling on the wrong side resulted in a general performance of consensus about what constituted a responsible life, when in fact there was, perhaps, no center at all.

For almost a year Elizabeth and Wes avoided naming the terms of their relationship. They celebrated the last night of 2011 with friends in the back of a truck, which they had rented for the night and converted into a mobile party, roaming around the city and stopping at bars along the way. They parked the truck before midnight outside a friend's apartment. Before going in, and because she wanted to say it while still relatively sober, Elizabeth told Wes she loved him. He loved her, too, but he still wanted sexual freedom. She had already decided she wanted it, too.

They agreed that they would think of themselves as a couple now instead of two single people who slept together, but they would still not be monogamous. Now they had to figure out how to manage the logistics. Elizabeth compiled a shared Google Document that was to become the foundation of their research—a syllabus of recommended reading, places to attend discussion groups, and sex parties open to the public—and Wes followed. He read the books that Elizabeth had read. They went to a play party at the sex club Mission Control, a floor-through apartment up a flight of stairs in a low-rise building on Mission Street. It was decorated with fake flowers, velvet paintings, Mexican doilies strung over the bar, a stripper pole, a "fungeon." They had sex surrounded by onlookers.

They returned another night, for an open-relationship discussion group, but most of the attendees were older, in their late thirties, and were either married and "frisky," or married and desperate to save their failing marriages. That was another thing about polyamory: at first almost none of their peers were trying it, at least not with the intention Wes and Elizabeth were showing. It was as if the precocity they showed in their professional lives extended into an extreme pragmatism about sex. I had met with other nonmonogamous communities in the Bay Area, who identified their sexuality with political aims such as anarchism and who sought to separate forms of love from government involvement. Elizabeth and Wes's inquiry was less about reconciling theory and practice. They did not speak of "the patriarchy," or quote Wilhelm Reich, but saw openness as the pursuit of honesty. They were seeking to avoid the confusion and euphemism of their generation's dating scene by talking through their real feelings, naming their actual desires, and having extensive uncomfortable conversations. Instead of facing the specter of commitment and running away in uncertainty, they would try to find a modified commitment that acknowledged their mutual desire for a more experiential life. Elizabeth and Wes felt they could draw upon certain ideas of the older polyamorists but had to do a lot of the thinking on their own. In monogamy there was one boundary. In their relationship there would be many. After completing their research they began to draw up rules.

The first held that on any given night, one could call the other and say, "Will you please come home." This rule served as a baseline: a shared understanding that each of them was the most important person in the other's life. The second rule was about disclosure. If one of them consciously suspected he or she might sleep with another person, the premonition or sentiment should be disclosed. They agreed to discuss each other's crushes. If a sexual encounter happened spontaneously, the event should be disclosed soon afterward. They would use condoms with their other partners. Despite making rules, they would aim to fail. It was a concept they borrowed from computer security: if an unplanned event occurs, what should the fallback response look like? In the "fail open mode," when an issue arises for which no rules or regulations have been devised, the default is to act first and discuss later, to have experiences first, then worry about formulating responses to those experiences for the next time.

The extrarelationship sex established a pattern. Elizabeth had more or less stable relationships. Wes was more likely to have one-night stands or meet with old friends while traveling for work. Wes did not tend to experience jealousy, although Elizabeth sometimes did.

In a final development, early in 2012, Brian left the country for three months. In the absence of her second partner, Elizabeth felt an imbalance. Wes was still dating other people and she felt precarious and vulnerable. She was also coming to terms with what had been a growing crush on someone else, another co-worker at Google. His name was Chris. He happened to be Wes's best friend.

Wes said he wouldn't mind if Elizabeth and Chris wanted to start sleeping together. Elizabeth, upset, asked how he could possibly care about her and want her to sleep with his best friend. They worked it out.

Chris is a tall man with a sweet smile and a shy affect. He grew up, like Elizabeth and Wes, with the expectation that happiness in life would be found in a long process of inquiry and experimentation. His parents had met at a commune in the hills of Santa Barbara in the early 1980s, so the example he had was one of youthful adventure that would eventually settle into conformity, if open-minded conformity—in suburban New Jersey, it turned out, where Chris grew up. For college he went west to Stanford, studied computer science and creative writing, and graduated, like Wes and Elizabeth, in 2010. He met Wes at Google, where they both started working later that year.

Chris and Wes became friends around the same time Wes met Elizabeth. Compared to them, Chris had more of an introspective personality. He wrote poetry. He was prone to occasional brooding. He did not have the easy emotional adjustment to the world around him that Elizabeth and Wes both had, and he was more careful about taking risks when it came to things like trying drugs and forming relationships.

The three of them spent time together at work, where they would regularly clock sixty or seventy hours a week, and by the end of 2011 they regularly socialized as a group outside of work, too. By early 2012, Chris and Elizabeth would also hang out by themselves, such as the time when they went to IKEA together, since he had a car and she didn't. Chris also knew, from conversations with them both, that his new friends were in an open relationship, but at first he saw his own role the way most single people feel with their couple friends: as a mutual confidant, a sort of child to two parents, with a much closer relationship to his male counterpart.

One night Chris accompanied Elizabeth and Wes to a queer dance party at the club Public Works, on Fourteenth and Mission. They went with a group, some co-workers from Google, some of Chris's friends from Stanford, and scattered representatives of Elizabeth's Burning Man crowd. Chris, Elizabeth, and Wes danced together, dancing that evolved seamlessly to making out on the dance floor. Chris enjoyed it, but felt a little bit like the third wheel. His friends were on MDMA and he was not (he had never liked MDMA, finding the crash of its aftermath, too psychologically destabilizing). Elizabeth and Wes had planned a foursome with another couple later that night, so Chris ended up going home alone.

But it was the first time the three of them had made out with one another, and soon making out with Elizabeth and Wes became a recurring event for Chris. Sometimes while sober, sometimes not, but it became an unspoken understanding that if the three of them went out dancing they would probably end up kissing together. This was true for a whole group of friends that began to coalesce at this time around Wes and Elizabeth, who began to be sought after as gurus by other couples their age who had considered opening their relationships. Elizabeth especially came to be known as someone to go to with questions. The shared Google Document soon had multiple subscribers. As the mood expanded, so did the openness.

One night Elizabeth came over to dinner at Chris's house, and after dinner decided to spend the night, much of which was spent awake and making out. The next day, Chris met with Wes. He asked Wes whether he really did not mind if he and Elizabeth occasionally slept together. Wes said that he truly did not mind. Then Chris brought up another idea. What about the three of them together, a group situation? he asked, carefully. And then: or just the two men?

Chris described himself as "mostly straight but every once in a while . . ." He had found his sexuality agreed with Alfred Kinsey's description of sexual orientation as a scale or spectrum. He had always assumed, when reading about the idea of the spectrum, that it meant a person had high levels of attraction to people of one gender and slightly lower levels to another. Instead, Chris had learned that he was attracted to many women and a few men but the strength of the attraction, to those to whom he was drawn, was the same regardless of gender. Wes happened to be one of the men to whom Chris was attracted. There had not been very many, so Chris was perhaps inclined to see the attraction as one of value and importance.

Wes, meanwhile, suspected that he was not gay at all, although in the spirit of the times was having trouble making such a closed-minded declaration. He told Chris he needed to think about it a bit.

Chris and Elizabeth began regularly sleeping with each other.

He continued his friendship with Wes. The two men were affectionate with each other, even kissing hello or goodbye, but the fact of his unreturned desire for Wes remained surprisingly difficult for Chris. It was harder to kill off his hopes than he had anticipated—and maybe Wes really *was* mulling over the idea.

Unlike some of the authors he read, Chris did not see monogamy as "unnatural" or imposed by some historical superstructure. He did not consider himself as having been "conditioned" toward some prescribed end. If there was a philosophical underpinning to his behavior it was that he considered himself a curious person. Some things he tried—sex with people of his own gender, psychoactive substances—because he wanted to be the kind of person who tried things. Wes and Elizabeth shared this view, too, that new experiences were valuable in themselves, even when they ended badly. If Chris felt left out, or Elizabeth got jealous, or Wes had to deal with uncomfortable sexual interest from his best friend, all of this was something to think about and explore rather than something to push away. They began to think of their three-way sexually charged friendship as a more advanced, if more difficult, form of relationship. It took on a purpose beyond personal satisfaction. It began to represent something better, a desire to improve human culture, to seek out a model of sexuality better suited to the present, to its freedoms, to its honesty.

Later, each of them in his or her own way would refer to this time as "the honeymoon period" or "the good part." Elizabeth even picked up an acronym, NRE, for New Relationship Energy. Nobody knew on a particular night how it was going to end. Chris still hoped that Wes might be a little bit gay. That spring of 2012, they were immersing in a new community, not just Chris, Elizabeth, and Wes, but an extended group who shared as a stated goal sexual openness with their partners and their friends.

I first met Chris, Elizabeth, and Wes around this time, in late May 2012, when their experiment was just a few months old. I was seven years older than Elizabeth and Chris and eight years older than Wes. I envied their community of friends, the openness with which they shared their attractions. Elizabeth, Wes, and Chris did not proceed recklessly. They drew up ethical codes to protect their relationships. They sought to protect emotions and physical health with rules and charters. They were earnest, without sarcasm or cynicism, and treated feelings as individual specimens, wrapped in cotton and carefully labeled. Instead of temptation as the ignoble emotion, jealousy was the reactionary response they tried never to indulge. My friend had been right: they were also self-confident, or at least Elizabeth and Wes seemed to plunge forward through life without fear. I saw in Chris a little more hesitation.

They were not bothered, as I was when I met them, by the evidence that nonmonogamous arrangements had ultimately been rejected by the last generation of straight people who had tried them. The experiments Elizabeth, Wes, and Chris were undertaking had a direct historic connection, in language and structure, to the sexual revolution. The 1960s and its immediate aftermath loomed over any practice of free love, as the last moment in living memory that my own particular demographic of Americans had initiated a massive and consequential critique of monogamy, especially as the last time that straight women had done intentional experiments in alternative lifestyles as part of a unified cultural movement. My moral worldview originated in that historical moment, along with my sexual freedom, the computers I used, my disinterest in organized religion, the multiculturalism I valued, and much of the literature and music I loved. It glowed from the past like a city just over the horizon.

My sense had always been that compared with people in the 1960s and '70s people my age had questioned very little about their expectations for adult life. I looked at the experiments of those decades and felt they had taught us that communes and other alternative arrangements that celebrated sexual freedom generally ended in jealousy and hurt feelings. Obedient children of the 1980s and '90s saw the failures of the counterculture, took them as implicit lessons from our parents, and held ourselves in thrall to grade point averages, drug laws, health insurance, student loan payments, college admissions, diplomas, internships, condoms, skin protection factors, antidepressants, designated smoking areas, politically correct language, child safety locks, gym memberships, cell phone contracts, bike helmets, cancer screenings, credit histories, and career advancement. We had a nuanced understanding of risk.

When it came to sex I thought we had it much better than they had. I thought of sex in the 1960s and '70s the way I thought of its contemporaries' drug use—they had gone to an unpleasant extreme, and now we knew better. They had done the work to sexually liberate women and start the gay rights movement, but we knew better than to move into rural communes or co-opt Native American spirituality or believe in Charles Reich's "Consciousness III" or force one's wife to sleep with another man to overcome her cultural programming. We had more access to birth control, and knew more about our bodies, and enjoyed greater gender equality in things like education and expectation, even if it didn't carry over into things like income equality or managerial power. We had a vast selection of vibrators sold in woman-friendly retail environments. We had *Sex and the City*.

We had AIDS and therefore had evolved a notion of "safer sex." We had rape crisis centers, legal abortion, and over-the-counter emergency contraception.

What my married parents imparted as the lessons from the 1960s was that it was fine to have as much casual ("safe") sex as we wanted as late-stage teenagers and young adults, and fine to secretly "experiment" with the more benign and least-addictive drugs (although no teacher or relative ever openly recommended it), but eventually we would grow up, stop using drugs, stop having sex with whomever we wanted, and settle into the nuclear families we saw on television, with an interlude in our twenties where we would live in cities with roommates. Some of us would be gay and that would be fine. Many of these families would fall apart, but we did not consider divorce a structural failure of an institution but a set of personal problems.

Haight-Ashbury by 1968, when my father arrived there—one summer late, it turned out—was a depressing place. If I doubted his word, I could read Joan Didion's "Slouching Towards Bethlehem." Or whoever—I pick Ellen Willis from a dozen possible writers who lived the time and came to the same conclusion, in her essay "Coming Down Again":

> Freedom is inherently risky, which is the reason for rules and limits in the first place; the paradox of the '60s generation is that we felt secure enough, economically and sexually, to reject security. The risks people took were real and so were the losses: the deaths, breakdowns, burnouts, addictions, the paranoia and nihilism, "revolutionary" crimes and totalitarian religious cults, poverty, and prison terms. Though the casualties of drugs and politics have been more conspicuous, sex has never been safe, certainly not for women and gay men: in a misogynist, homophobic culture suffused with sexual rage, to be a "whore"

or a "pervert" is to "ask for" punishment. [From *The Essential Ellen Willis*, University of Minnesota Press, 2014.]

So people my age believed in rules, even if they were not always obeyed. We risked less, but we also expected to suffer less punishment. I saw this as a kind of enlightenment. The nuclear families on television now showed interracial and same-sex couples. We had expanded our idea of normal. We therefore needed no science-fictional overhaul, no modified futuristic family model where we designated marriage as situated on the wrong side of history and raised our children in communal crèches guarded over by free-loving communitarians or, as Arthur C. Clarke predicted in 1953 in *Childhood's End*, signed limited marriage contracts of five to ten years. That was what the 1960s had taught us: not to tamper with the fundamental structures of the family and society. Even in the attempt to establish a conflict between gay sex and marriage, marriage would ultimately win.

Marriage was the one word in our era of sexual freedom that had not lost its specificity. In contrast to the linguistic murk of *dating* we still knew what *marriage* meant: a lifelong commitment, both sexual and familial, to another person. To be married in life was in perfect congruence with what it meant to be married on one's tax form.

Among my mostly secular group of friends the ceremonies of marriage and death were the only ritual sacraments left. In those years I went to weddings in rural Vermont, New Orleans, Los Angeles, and Quebec. I went to weddings in Lisbon, Chicago, Brooklyn, and upstate New York. Most of my travel and spending money went toward weddings. They reminded me that there was one sexual relationship still governed by strict rules. People who married believed in commitment. Most of them believed they could uphold monogamy. They planned to purchase single-family homes and eventually bear children. They wanted to care for each other when old.

This is not to say that the weddings I attended confidently asserted the institution of marriage. In marrying each other, my friends wanted to prove they had not succumbed to institutional conformity at the very moment they asserted their institutional conformity. They didn't want to cop out entirely, they didn't want to blindly mimic a housewife-patriarch dynamic, but they wanted to move into the more stable sphere of adult existence. These neo-marriages therefore had to be an expression of the purest love and show a deliberate break with history. I went to Catholic weddings, Jewish weddings, and Hindu weddings, but cultural tradition was often merely aesthetic adornment or enacted with perfunctory deference to please relatives. In many cases there was no ceremony, religious or otherwise. Just enough was included to add a patina of history without having to suffocate under history's predilections toward intolerance. At other times the elimination of traditional wedding usage and terms was presented in apologetic solidarity with those communities who were until very recently denied marriage. The rise of "partner" over "husband" or "wife" was increasingly mainstream, a successful linguistic flattening of hierarchies of sexual orientation, gender, and marital status. This made lots of sense in a business or professional context, but less sense, perhaps, with family and friends, where it begged the question of what marriage is worth, if not a public declaration of the nature of one's relationship to another person, and what equality is worth, if it demands the total obfuscation of the differences between humans.

The care my friends took to separate their marriages from the history of marriage tacitly acknowledged a recently agreed-upon truth: marriage should not mean one person losing her independence, her name, and her autonomy to another. Having sought to eliminate this subjugation, we now tried to convince ourselves that marriage between men and women could carry the nice parts of its history without its gendered roles. Its mystique survived its reformation, and its well-documented downsides would still ennoble us: even my most sexually adventurous friends remained willing to risk the hypocrisy, dishonesty, diminished sexual desire, or mute unhappiness of many marriages.

I did not doubt the nobility of such malaise. I believed in the mystique of commitment—that, as Beauvoir had once sarcastically described it, "routine takes on the cast of adventure; fidelity, that of a sublime passion; ennui becomes wisdom; and family hatred is the deepest form of love." I could conceive of no viable alternative; the options I could name were alien to me: open marriages, swingers, polyamory . . . But this left a vacuum of ideas for any future of sustainable sexuality outside of a narrative that culminated in marriage. Could I think of myself as an adult if I never married? Would my married friends become distant and remote? Was there a way to imagine a sexual relationship beyond the linear progression of a "relationship"? In between weddings I entered the homes of monogamous couples who lived together. They would feed me and introduce me to their pets and later their babies. I looked for guidance in their towels and coverlets, the organization of the shared closet, their cake stands or seltzer machines and houseplants. I would enter the home of an ex-boyfriend now living with a woman and experience even greater estrangement, looking at the hairpins on the glass shelf below the medicine cabinet, or the flaxseed oil in the refrigerator. This was the life he had chosen over our life together, which would have had different hair accessories, no flaxseed oil in the refrigerator. "I don't know how to pin up my hair properly," I would think, as an explanation.

To stop thinking of marriage as the only feasible resolution to the question of what my sexual future might look like I had to at least consider polyamory, open relationships, and the other phenomena, to start seeing the changes not as threats to the ideal relationship but as ideals in themselves. Elizabeth, Wes, and Chris believed there were still primary choices to make about sexuality. They saw occasionally taking psychedelics and MDMA as a way to suspend some of the suspicions and phobias that made consideration of such choices difficult. I thought that parade had already gone by, that it had ended with the Manson Family. I thought the secondhand sexual freedom passed down by my parents had been sufficient to my needs, until I realized it wasn't. Nonmonogamy—or rather, free love—as an organizing principle of sexuality, adopted en masse and recognized in language and law, would break with history, which was why it was such a popular theme in science fiction. Like outer space, the prospect of free love was always there, humans just had to figure out how to make it hospitable to our needs. I wasn't the only one who kept thinking about the warnings of people who had observed the 1960s and felt hesitation. There was a phrase being thrown around the Bay Area only half-jokingly: "responsible hedonism."

In the spring of 2012, Elizabeth would spend most nights with Wes, and the occasional night with Chris or someone else. The three friends would see one another at work, too, staying late and having meals together in the cafeteria. When their relationships evolved, the shifts tended to happen not in slow increments but with sudden tectonic upheavals, usually during out-of-town retreats that served as emotional crucibles, where the suspension of the usual barriers to human emotion, often through experimentation with psychoactive substances, would provoke the revelation of suppressed feeling. Chris later contemplated writing an essay called "2012: A Story of Sex, Love, and MDMA." The essay would be punctuated by a series of parties: New Year's Eve, the night the three first made out at Public Works, and now, as summer approached, other events.

The decision to go to the Electric Daisy Carnival in Las Vegas was originally made with the intention of having a semi-ironic reconnaissance with the mainstream. EDC was a corporate perversion of rave culture, a party with none of the do-it-yourself communal values that guided the partying of their group of friends. Still, it was probably going to be funny, and if not they would make it funny, so that June the three lovers and some thirty of their friends booked a block of rooms at Planet Hollywood and flew to Las Vegas.

The festival took place at the Las Vegas Speedway on the outskirts of town. One hundred thousand people were in attendance, and the traffic from the strip to the speedway, normally a fifteen-minute drive, took two hours. The friends from San Francisco had chartered a bus to take them to and from the event. It quickly became clear that their bus driver pointedly hated them. He pulled over the bus in a fury to rage about their drug use, would take directions only from the men in the group, and saw some national problem embodied in these young, handsome professionals dressed androgynously in Day-Glo.

Another downer came on the Saturday night of the festival, when high winds forced the music to shut down at one a.m., stranding the thousands of ravers who had carefully calculated their milligrams and micrograms for at least another five hours of dancing. The San Francisco group, their own reality somewhat distorted, carefully made their way to the bleachers overlooking the speedway and watched the scene unfold like a weather event on television: organizers attempting to corral confused herds in furries and blinky lights hither and yon; an unfounded rumor that the festival would be reopening at a specific entry point, prompting a multicolored swarm.

These were logistical problems, but Chris felt depressed for other reasons. EDC, of all places—it was supposed to be a joke! EDC was where some truths about his relationship with Elizabeth and Wes were being revealed. Elizabeth preferred to say that EDC was when Chris realized "Wes and I liked each other and our relationship was real." If Chris thought the three of them had taken on an adventure on equal footing, he now saw that it was not quite that way. They were adventuring as a couple. He was on his own.

When they got back to San Francisco, Elizabeth went to London for a couple of weeks for work. Wes simply disappeared, ignoring Chris's calls, doing his own thing, work or something else. Chris felt abandoned.

Chris and Wes never had the deep discussions about feelings that Elizabeth and Chris had. When they passed through an intermediary period during which Chris was feeling left out, it manifested more as a general, unacknowledged tension between the friends than an actual rift. When Chris was happier, the tension would fade, and the two men would be friends again.

Elizabeth had only a vague idea about Chris's difficulties. He did not tell them a lot in the moment. Elizabeth knew he wanted emotional intimacy, and that he liked them a lot. She liked him a lot, too, but she also knew there would never be a complete three-way match. It was not that she could not picture herself as part of a triad, but she knew that Wes would never be a part of such an arrangement.

The summer passed with a certain degree of estrangement, everyone punching in excess hours at Google. At summer's end, the last week before Labor Day, Chris and Wes joined Elizabeth for her second Burning Man and the three decided to share a tent. The first day was spent setting up their camp, in whiteout dust storm conditions. The second day of the festival was so-called Molly Make Out Monday for their theme camp. MDMA had never been a good drug for Chris—at EDC he had avoided it— but hey, it was Burning Man. He told himself he would be fine. He told himself he wanted to do it. Instead of the hot-water-bottle warmth of low-grade empathogenic softness, Chris felt like all the Adderall, coffee beans, green teas, and Diet Cokes he had ingested in a lifetime were converging somewhere in his torso, his brain reduced to spinning hamster wheels and the relentless pulse of blinking lights moving in rhythm with electronic dance music. Having taken extra care to stay hydrated, he drank too much water, and thirty-six hours into Burning Man, Chris was doubled over outside the phantasmagoric dance party at Opulent Temple, vomiting, panicking, and wishing he were anywhere else.

The third day he spent lying in the shade.

He had hoped for, and been told about, the likelihood of having a profound emotional experience at Burning Man. He had countered this expectation with an internal dialogue, that all that was "phooey," that he was simply attending an elaborate party in the desert, that he was not the sort to have intense emotional experiences, and that he was in it for the party. He ended up having a profound emotional experience, he just hadn't supposed it would be so terrible. He remembered, for example, that he does not like talking to strangers. Riding his dolled-up bicycle through the dust and heat, he experienced the dissonance of the tourist in a foreign environment, as if he had landed not at Burning Man but in rural China, where people were all around, each person with his or her own place in the universe, but he was profoundly alone, separated by a barrier of insurmountable isolation.

One thing, however, proved heartening about the experience. In the end, despite the difficulties, Burning Man restored the balance of friendship among the three of them. On Molly Make Out Monday, it was Wes and Elizabeth who cared for Chris the whole night he was ill. They helped him work through his feelings of isolation. Once again, the hurt feelings were submerged. Elizabeth and Wes might be together, but they cared about him, too.

The feelings did not go away completely, however. Chris watched as Elizabeth and Wes grew closer and closer to each other. He returned to San Francisco after Burning Man with the intention of developing a serious relationship of his own. After all the heady uncertainty he wanted quiet and stability, but if anything, things were going in the opposite direction. He dated some women, nothing stuck, and his desire for a longer-term commitment had no bearing on the dating he was doing, where he didn't meet anybody he loved.

At the end of 2012, a year into their heightened friendship, the three of them took another weekend trip together. This time they drove down the coast to San Luis Obispo. They had booked a room at the Madonna Inn, a kitschy old hotel on the side of the 101. (Elizabeth, Wes, and Chris might have avoided irony in discussing sexuality, but they embraced it in their choice of weekend getaways.) It rained the whole weekend, so they spent it talking, surrounded by pink rose carpets and stone fireplaces, brass rails and chintz. They talked, but as if everyone agreed that Chris was pleased with his status as moonlighting lover, which he wasn't. They were three best friends with a clear division, a distance he felt acutely. Afterward, he went to Santa Barbara, where his parents now lived, for the holidays. He compared his state of mind that Christmas with that of Superman in his Fortress of Solitude.

Wes and Elizabeth's relationship had acquired an acceleration, a momentum based on mutual daring. In the beginning, Elizabeth had devised the rules and regulations of the relationship out of fear. She had wanted to cover all of her bases, guard each of her possible weaknesses, and outline every parameter. After a year of nonmonogamy had passed, she had learned that preventing conflict was less important than resolving it. By 2013, the rules of a more uncertain phase of commitment began to drop away. The more solid their relationship, the more adventurous she could be.

In the way that some couples might spend their energy systematically researching and eating at new restaurants in a city, Elizabeth and Wes went to sex parties. Elizabeth attended two porn shoots at Kink, one of them with Wes, another with a woman who had become another long-term sexual partner. In June 2013, Wes left Google to start his own company. Between ending the one job and beginning the other, he traveled around Europe. Elizabeth met him in Amsterdam, where they decided to take advantage of legal sex work and hire a prostitute.

Chris kept dating. He dated one woman for two months, another woman for four months. Dating people felt quiet and uncomplicated. It felt basic but also boring, like nothing was at stake. He no longer worried about explaining his sexual arrangements with the people he dated—everyone in San Francisco now seemed to assume they were in open relationships. So Chris kept sleeping with Elizabeth, too, but still with some worry. In May 2013, Elizabeth needed to take a work trip to Tokyo. Chris decided to go with her and play "house husband." It proved to be another turning point, of sorts.

They stayed at the Ritz-Carlton overlooking the Tokyo

cityscape. Elizabeth worked during the day, and Chris wandered the city and the hotel by himself. On their last night in Tokyo, a Friday, after Elizabeth's professional duties had ended for the week, they sat down across from each other and each took a tab of LSD.

They stayed up all night, talking. For Elizabeth, as for Chris, their relationship reached its most honest state that spring night, overlooking the glittering expanse of Tokyo. The previous year had been a long series of failures in communication, conversations that felt impossible because they demanded exposure of the deep vulnerabilities.

For the first time they honestly discussed Chris's understanding of Wes, of how in Chris's hopes and expectations he had fallen in love, "filled in the dots with his own lines," as Elizabeth put it, and perhaps avoided acknowledging aspects of Wes's personality that empirically contradicted Chris's idea of him. They talked about Elizabeth's optimism, and Chris's pessimism, how pessimistic people might also be better at accurately assessing their reality. Elizabeth left the conversation feeling they finally understood their differences, but also felt Chris's romantic attraction to her break.

When they talked about their co-workers in the Bay Area, Chris and Wes discussed the culture of "hyperbolic optimism," which they defined as a genuine commitment to the idea that all things were possible. It was not a tenable ideology, was in fact totally ungrounded in any wider reality, but for a number of reasons hyperbolic optimism could actually be pondered in the highly specific time and place of San Francisco, in the first half of the second decade of the new millennium, among a group of young educated people with high standards of living. Chris saw it in the hubris of Ross Ulbricht, the founder of Silk Road, the Internet marketplace whose founding premise was that being good at navigating the Internet meant one could, from the humble confines of Glen Park Library, defy a whole range of federal laws. He saw it in the "nontrivial" number of his co-workers who genuinely believed there was a reasonable chance they would live forever, who read the works of Ray Kurzweil and made plans for the singularity. He saw it in his friends, who saw no reason not to try going beyond sexual traditions that had governed societal behavior for thousands of years. Few people, he noticed, bothered with the question of whether one would really *want* to live forever.

The hyperbolic optimists, as Chris saw it, thought that an action was right if it promoted individual happiness, regardless of its effect on others. Radical selfishness was an easy philosophy for a group of people who did not really have any problems, who made lots of money and had socially progressive and flexible work environments. His friends were not libertarians, but the way they approached sex had roots in a libertarian idea that if the right dynamics were set up every problem would work itself out. As Chris learned, this ignored the element of human emotion involved in figuring things out. But while he recognized the reality distortion of the hyperbolic optimists, he wasn't setting himself entirely apart from their outlook. His experiences had not led him to retrench into monogamy. Monogamy also "didn't work." The only way to go was forward. By 2014, Chris was in a serious relationship. They agreed to still sleep with other people, when moved to do so.

As untraditional as Wes and Elizabeth's relationship was, it had started to look like it was heading toward the traditional happy ending. They met, they slowly fell in love. They discussed moving in together over the course of a year, and finally did so in late

2013. Wes felt that being open made the process of declaring a serious commitment easier. The decision to move in together carried less weight with the knowledge that at least a few nights a month one of them would be spending the night at someone else's place. They both liked that being apart from each other became a structural part of their relationship, and that reasons for spending time alone did not have to be manufactured and excused. The lingering question, for both Elizabeth and Wes, was what would happen should one of them fall in love with someone else. If they continued together into the future, then there would be times when they would fall in love with other people they were dating. They even discussed this likelihood with an older married couple, a couple in their late thirties who had been married for years and open for longer than Elizabeth and Wes had been dating. The man told them a story of how in the course of their open marriage his wife had truly fallen for another person. He called it a "crisis episode" in their marriage. Her love for the other person was real but they decided together that they were what they called "life journey partners"—a designation that sounded very hokey, but which was meant to indicate, said Wes, that "there's being in love and there's being in love and wanting to spend the rest of your life with someone." There would be times when a person had to compromise.

In August 2014, while at Burning Man, Elizabeth and Wes got engaged. In August 2015, I attended their wedding in Black Rock City. They encouraged their guests to dress as bridesmaids, and women and men wore wigs, thrift store prom dresses, and lacy hats. To the tune of "Somewhere over the Rainbow" played on an electric piano, Wes and Elizabeth, he in a white button-down shirt and black trousers, she in a white dress, both with colorful face paint around their eyes, processed to an altar decorated with pink fabric flowers and tasseled fringe. Relatives delivered loving statements. Wes's godfather recited a Druid prayer. Elizabeth's best friend recited a poem by Derrick Brown called "A Finger, Two Dots, and Me" ("The design / in the stars / is the same / in our hearts.")

Elizabeth and Wes, who were close to all four of their parents, had told them about their polyamory. "A successful marriage involves falling in love many times . . . always with the same person," said Wes's dad, in his speech, and the audience laughed knowingly.

Wes and Elizabeth spoke in turn. "When I was little I had to learn how to relate to others," said Wes. His way of connecting, he said, was to "ask for big numbers from friends to show off at long division." He thanked the people who had shown him love even when he didn't know how to reciprocate. Elizabeth had taught him how to love, he said. He spoke of their shared pursuit of communitarianism, "that there is no coherent notion of humans as ethical actors outside their culture and tribe; that humans have an ethical obligation to contribute to their communities and the right to be supported in turn in times of need." He called Elizabeth "my strongest attractor in this great space we're all living in."

"When I told him I loved him he responded just like Han Solo responded to Princess Leia: 'I know,'" said Elizabeth, when it was her turn. She spoke of her excitement at planning a future in years rather than months, of looking forward to the children they would have together.

Chris sat grinning in the audience, next to his girlfriend. When he stood up to speak he recalled the early days of their friendship, "a period when we were exploring whether love and intimacy can be freely given." He recalled his rocky first experience at Burning Man, and when he traveled to Japan with Elizabeth and realized "it wasn't me she needed, it was Wes, back home." He grew introspective, evoking his desire to seek new ways of being in the world. "When I'm looking for relationships that are stronger I don't have to look very far," he said.

Wes and Elizabeth shared their vows privately, while their friends and family stood around them in a ring. We lit sparklers and held them skyward as the sun set, forming a ring of light. The drone of a didgeridoo obscured the couple's quiet murmuring. We stood there, sparklers lifted, standing on the soft dust, until we held only thin and smoking pieces of metal and dusk fell over us. "By the power invested in me by the Internet, you are now married," said the officiant, Wes's uncle. "You can kiss each other and other people."

Chris and Elizabeth threw their first sex party together in the fall of 2012. The idea was to throw a sex party that was actually cool, with people whom they liked, so they didn't feel like a bunch of married swingers in a room listening to "Don't You Want Me, Baby." In early 2015 I went to the fourth iteration of the event: Thunderwear IV. It was held in a rented loft south of Market Street. A photographer had taken photographs of Elizabeth, and a black-and-white portrait of her lifting one of her legs up over her head in a full split and penetrating herself with a dildo hung over the room. She had also installed a stripper pole.

The invitation had laid out the party's rules in a charter, to which every invitee had to agree:

1. Useful mantra: low expectations, high possibilities.
2. Consent is required. And sexy. If you wanna do
    something, ask first. Bonus points for enthusiastic consent.
3. This is a party. Parties are fun! You don't have to do

anything you don't wanna do. If you don't wanna, say "no thanks."

4. This is a party. Have fun! White ribbon means: ask to feed me (remember, you can say no). Red ribbon means: ask me for a kiss (on the cheek . . . at first at least ;)

5. Relationship conversation with your partner recommended <u>before</u> you start partying.

A final rule: no glitter, at the request of the venue.

As guests arrived, they were asked to read the charter, then were given bracelets of red and white satin cord. The party started calmly: drinking and talking, like any other party. Wes made me a vodka and cranberry juice; I stood and talked with one of the two other people at the party over the age of thirty. Some people wore street clothes, like me. Others changed into special outfits: Wes in white sparkly boy shorts and a black shirt; Elizabeth in leather shorts and knee-high boots. One woman wore a red thrift shop dress accessorized with a leather corset, another had a leather corset that left her breasts bare. Another man wore gold leggings with a fur coat. A woman wearing a fish-net bodysock had a rhinestone choker that spelled s-e-x across her throat. Elizabeth, ever organized, told me she had purchased liability insurance for the stripper pole.

Among themselves, the friends had arranged to begin the evening with an amateur burlesque show. We watched a slightly botched silk acrobatic routine to the song "Jump" by Rihanna. The dancer's foot kept slipping out of her toehold and she would need to rewind the silk and harness herself back in. "She isn't very good at it," sighed the woman standing next to me, who, like me, was more of an interloper among what was mostly a group of good friends, and also in her mid-thirties. The rest of the group clapped and whooped encouragingly. The next woman performed a pirate-themed striptease that concluded with her taping a pair of red Solo cups to her breasts, filling them with Malibu, orange juice, and coconut milk, and letting people drink from them with straws. Then, to Rihanna's "Birthday Cake," came a striptease that ended with the performer smearing herself all over with cake. Then we watched a professional pole-dancing instructor perform a poignant dance to the song "Wildest Moments" by Jessie Ware.

After the show, I wandered around. The loft gave way to a second large room with a couch and two king-size beds made up with satin sheets. I walked into the massive slate-gray bathroom with its Jacuzzi and had a conversation with a couple about the dream of one day living in a backyard casita in Oakland with a composting toilet. I wandered back outside to the loft, where couples and threesomes had begun to pair off on couches. The party was vaguely food themed, so there were chocolate-covered strawberries in one corner. Nearby was a wheel of fortune that could be spun for different instructions. After several conversations with other single people, conversations that felt like job interviews, I ended up taking turns spinning the wheel of fortune with a man. I did so with a slightly exhausted determination to get the show on the road. He was a bit younger. We spun the wheel, awkwardly obeying the instructions to feed each other chocolate-covered strawberries and kiss. Then we went into the second room to do whip-its. I had never done a whip-it.

My new friend explained how it worked: screw on a small canister of nitrous oxide to the stainless-steel whipped-cream maker. Exhale deeply, then inhale while depressing the handle of the machine, filling your lungs with nitrous oxide instead of oxygen. This produces a short, one- or two-minute high. Deprived of oxygen, the mind dissolves; physical sensation becomes acute, a goofy giddiness and bubbliness sets in. Whip-its are good for a sex party because they do not impair sexual function and can heighten physical sensation, although I was advised not to do too many because, said Elizabeth, "it starts to become difficult to come back."

On my first whip-it, the man I had met lightly touched my arm while I lay back, the feeling of his hands producing warmth and electricity while my vision broke into geometric patterns. During his turn, he asked that I kiss him. We made out for a while, doing the occasional whip-it, the cold, cheerfully colored canisters accumulating in the folds of the sheets we lay on. I felt airy and happy. We stood up with our hands against the wall and took turns doing whip-its and smacking each other with a riding crop. Around us, groups of people lay together on beds and couches, stood making out in corners. On a couch, a man lay across the laps of his friends, who formed a spanking train. The room filled with the pneumatic sound of whip-its and of the metal canisters rolling across the floor. I sat with Elizabeth and took a whip-it, after which she massaged my head while a man lightly shocked me with an electrified wand.

The after party was at the apartment of one of Elizabeth's partners, a man with whom she had exchanged I-love-yous. I had overheard a conversation between her and Wes before she left, where she had asked Wes if he would let her go on her own. It was a conversation that was difficult to listen to. I believed Wes when he cheerfully assented, but I also knew my own feelings would have been hurt. Chris was there, too, with his now-steady girlfriend.

The after party was held in the penthouse of a new building. Its windows looked over the LED light installation on the Bay Bridge, the cars speeding back to Oakland for the night under icicles of white light, fewer coming to San Francisco from the other direction. The apartment felt unlived in, all glossy surfaces and wood, the refrigerators in drawers, a bowl of small apples that were uniform in shape and color. The master bedroom had the impractical bathroom of an overdesigned hotel, with no door, just an open alcove off to one side. On the whiteboard of the office, an app had been carefully diagrammed, like a stage set, and what books there were on the shelves were ordered by height. Elizabeth had slyly slipped me a condom but I didn't have sex. I had a boyfriend in New York, and he had not wanted me to attend the party at all. Elizabeth said she knew people who were good at counseling about how to open a relationship if both people did not share the same interest in it, but I was still thinking of myself as just a visitor, or rather neither here nor there, someone undertaking an abstract inquiry but not yet with true intention. I regretted having been shy in my making out earlier at the sex party, that I had spent the night with one person instead of joining the cuddle puddle that had coalesced on the satin-sheeted bed opposite. I wished I had other chances for this degree of experimentation, and wondered what it would feel like not to be a visitor to this scene, but a part of it. It had been easier for me to relax because most of the people in the room had been strangers. Had they been my friends, I would have been self-conscious. Now I sat in the office with a group of sleepy partygoers. We chatted and looked at the view of the bridge and the unceasing exchange of cars. In the background was the sound of whip-its, of orgasms, of water falling from a shower into a porcelain tub.

BURNING MAN

I wanted to go to Burning Man because I saw the great festival in the desert as the epicenter of the three things that interested me most in 2013: sexual experimentation, psychedelic drugs, and futurism. But everyone said Burning Man was over, that it was spoiled. It was inundated with rich tech people who defied the festival's precious tenet of radical self-reliance by their overreliance on paid staff. Burning Man, which started in 1986 when twenty people burned an effigy on the beach, was turning into a dusty version of Davos. It was the kind of thing Ashton Kutcher went to, and the wife of the Aga Khan, and they came only to gawk, not to participate. Old-timers lamented the rise of "plug and play" culture. The community had gotten mainstream. There were too many LEDs now, too many RVs, too many generators, tech executives, and too much EDM. There were TED talks. There were technolibertarians.

I would decide for myself. I rented an RV with six other

people, a group organized by a friend in San Francisco. I think if someone were to draw a portrait of the people who were "ruining Burning Man" it would have looked like us. With one exception the six all worked in the tech industry. The exception was a corporate lawyer. None of us had been to Burning Man before. We paid a company from San Diego to drive our RV to Nevada and pack out our trash afterward.

I ordered all the things online: dust goggles, sunscreen, sun hat, headlamp, some LED lights, animal print leggings. I arranged delivery of a bicycle. My friends would bring the food and water from San Francisco. I wondered about how to get drugs to Nevada, and decided it was safest to show up and hope someone would provide.

Meanwhile, my fellow RV crowd delayed their planning with the last-minute flexibility of people who don't worry about money. They bought plane tickets at the last minute, and then changed their flights. One of them still had not gotten a ticket two days before he was supposed to go. One of them ordered a bicycle from eBay Now and had it delivered to his San Francisco office within an hour, like a taco. One of them ended up flying the hundred miles from Reno to Black Rock City in a chartered Cessna.

I flew to Reno using frequent-flyer miles and stood by a folding table at the airport until someone offered me a ride. He was a dad from Greenwich, Connecticut, who worked in finance. He also gave a ride to a medieval literature scholar from Chicago. The finance guy had once had another job, engineering teledildonics at the turn of the new century. On the way through the empty desert landscape, speeding toward the prehistoric lakebed where Burning Man is held each year, we smoked concentrate of weed through an electronic vaporizer shaped like an elegant black kazoo. We talked about teledildonics and hexayurts.

We arrived at the gate to Black Rock City just after sunset.

We listened to a dedicated radio station, which ordered us in a stern voice to drive ten miles an hour. We waited in line for two hours. Outside, people got in and out of their cars. They drank beers. Caravans communicated with each other by walkie-talkie under the floodlights. On the horizon we could see the festival, multicolored and twinkling. This year 68,000 people had come to Burning Man. Thirteen years ago, when the finance guy from Greenwich had come for the first time, there had been 15,000 attendees. One of my car mates, who was from Mexico, observed that the scene was just like the U.S.-Mexico border, especially when, at the entrance, our car was searched for stowaways. We handed over our tickets. We hugged the greeters, lay on our backs and made snow angels in the dust, and rang a bell. We had arrived.

Burning Man is organized in circles, like Dante's Inferno. The circles, letters A through L, are intersected by minutes, like a clock. Most people stay at theme camps, which combine collective infrastructure—kitchen, sun showers, shade, water tanks—with individual dwellings. These range from high-end operations with a full catering service to groups of friends from California and Nevada with common sexual, political, musical, or professional interests camping in tents. The themes could be creative—one camp, Animal Control, was dedicated to trapping and tagging Burning Man attendees in animal costumes. Others served coffee every morning, or played only music by the Grateful Dead.

Because we were radically reliant on some people from San Diego to provide us with an RV and had waited until the last minute to plan our attendance, we were not with a camp. Instead we were placed on the outermost circle, at L and 7:00, next to the guy who had driven fifteen RVs from San Diego to Burning Man. His name was Jesus. He showed me around the RV. He was very drunk. Speaking English with a Spanish accent, he talked about his homesickness, how he was tired of being here and excited to go home, to Minnesota, where he lived. We talked about Minnesota, where I had grown up. He showed me various stowaway beds in which the seven of us could sleep, then pressed a button to expand the RV in width. In the process, an open medicine-cabinet door was ripped off its hinges. Its mirror shattered on the floor. "I'll clean it up," said Jesus, scooping piles of broken glass with his bare hands.

I biked out to the playa, the central area where things happen at night. I passed awesome structures, orbited by glowing people on other bikes. I biked back around the outer streets of Black Rock City, which were deserted and dark. I was lonely. I did not yet understand how to interact with this place. I returned to the RV, found it still empty, and went out again. I watched an animatronic octopus spit fire from its articulated metal limbs to the rhythm of electronic dance music. I climbed the spaceship with the Burning Man on top. I returned to the RV. I hoped my friends would arrive soon.

They arrived after three a.m. I say "my friends" but I knew only one of them, Adam, and him I barely knew. Earlier in the summer we had spent a week together in Portugal after hooking up at a wedding. The last time I saw him had been at seven a.m. in Lisbon, when he left my bed to catch an airplane to a bachelor party in Austin, Texas. Now we reunited in the middle of the night in the Nevada desert. Other than sex we had little in common. "We have nothing in common!" we would marvel.

He lived in San Francisco and worked in tech. He was always "slammed" at work. Judging from his social media feeds he attended lots of conferences with "thought leaders," destination weddings, ski trips, holidays with groups of friends in beautiful houses, and he was frequently launching new initiatives with his rapidly expanding company. He had subscribed to a DNA mapping service that predicts how you might die, the results of which are posted to an iPhone app, so that your iPhone knows how likely you are to get heart disease. When the subject of Burning Man first came up, we both talked about how we wanted to go, how we knew people made fun of it but that we were drawn to it. He said he saw it as a good networking opportunity, but we also saw it as a thing that was happening right now and only right now, and we were both interested in things that were specific to the present.

Now he put on a reflective jumpsuit and a fedora. We ate some caramel-corn marijuana purchased from a California medical dispensary, went out until dawn, then came back to the RV and had sex, despite the other occupants of the RV. "I want to have sex with this person forever," I thought afterward.

It took me thirty-six hours to get adjusted to Burning Man. During that time I was aware that something was happening around me, in which I could partake, but I did not know how to begin. The greeters at the gate had given us a guidebook, called "What Where When," which listed events that read like mini prose poems in futurist jargon. "NEW TECH CITY SOCIAL INNOVATION FUTURES," read one. "Creative autonomous zones & cities of the future . . . resiliency, thrivability, open data, mixing genomes and biometrics with our passwords and crypto-currencies. What's your future look like? Social entrepreneurs and free culture makers, hack the system and mash the sectors." For someone interested in sexual experimentation, the opportunities for self-education here were endless: there were lectures on orgasmic meditation, "shamanic auto-asphyxiation," eco-sexuality, "femtheogens," "tantra of our menses," "sex drugs and electronic music," and the opportunity to visit the orgy dome.

I biked around, accepted offers of lemonade and drinks, and

had some conversations. I attended a lecture on new research about treating illnesses with psychedelic drugs. I listened to someone describe her dissertation, "Transpersonal Phenomena Induced by Electronic Dance Music." The weed made Adam excitable and inattentive. Next to his bed, a small landfill of plastic water bottles had accumulated. I wasn't sure if he wanted to hang out with me, or share his life-hacked body with the naked free spirits of Burning Man. I wasn't sure what I wanted. The second night, to give everyone space, I biked over to the outer playa, where it was silent, empty, and very cold. I went to bed early.

The next day I woke up around nine a.m. I went out alone and walked past a plywood booth painted yellow. Its sign advertised "Non-Monogamy Advice." A rainbow flag blew taut in the wind, the words "Yes Please" printed on it in white. Beneath that was a black flag with a pirate's skull and crossbones. Signs hung on the booth said the doctor was "curious" and "available," but I didn't see anyone. I went closer to read the articles taped to the booth, which claimed humans had not evolved to be monogamous.

As I stood there squinting a sleepy-looking tall man with a shaved head ambled forth from beneath a tent, holding an enameled metal cup of coffee. He was sunburned and blue-eyed and spoke with a northern European accent. He sat down on the other side of the booth. I sat facing him. The sun beat down. "Would you like an umbrella?" he asked. Two umbrellas were leaned against the advice booth. He opened a rainbow umbrella and I opened a black one and we now looked at each other from beneath our umbrellas. I took off my sunglasses.

"Do you have a question?" he asked.

I didn't. I told him that my last relationship had ended two years ago. I supposed that since then I had been nonmonogamous, in the sense of sometimes having sex with several different people within a specific period of time. As I said this both the idea of counting people and the idea of grouping them within a time frame seemed arbitrary. This was just my life: I lived it and sometimes had sex with people. Sometimes I wanted to commit to people, or they to me, but in the past two years no such interests had fallen into alignment. Once I had gone about this behavior more or less by accident, still thinking that I would find someone to love and start a relationship. Now I sought out sex even when it would lead nowhere. I thought of it as a way to become closer to people who intrigued me, whom I wanted to understand better. It was always a surprise, the differences between the people with whom I shared a physical connection and those with whom I connected on the level of ideas. But there were still some problems, I said.

I still did not feel as free as I wanted to. Sometimes I could not cross the barriers that keep people from expressing their desires. Rejection did not hurt any less, although it did not hurt more, and I knew better now how to work through it, by trying to accept the rejection as an honest expression of the other person's feelings, not as a negative verdict on who I was or had failed to be, and that pursuing sex with other people really could help me reconnect with the world after heartbreak. Sometimes, in sexual relationships that would only ever be casual, my nerve would fail me or a grasping would set in. It was still difficult to get from point A to point B with total ease, despite all of the facilitators specifically designed for that purpose on the touch screen of my mobile phone.

I said all this to the guru. He took a sip of his coffee. The day was starting to warm. I had no practical questions. I tried to think of problems. I asked him about jealousy.

"Jealousy is something you have to feel," he said. "I don't try to argue it away, or pretend it isn't happening. I just sink into it."

He was from the Netherlands. He had been in a polyamorous relationship that had ended when he realized he and his girlfriend no longer loved each other. Maybe polyamory was just a slower way of breaking up with someone. I considered that perhaps it was a more humane way of breaking up with someone and that anyway, in most relationships, at most times, both people can already fathom how the relationship will end. Eventually I put on my sunglasses, closed my umbrella, and stood up to continue walking. The streets were still mostly deserted. It was early for Black Rock City.

I walked past a library. I went in and sat down and started looking at the broadsheet daily newspaper that someone prints during Burning Man. The issue I read was from Wednesday. Today was Friday. A caption described people falling off a sculpture of a coyote. Across from me a man with dark hair and black glasses sat looking through a stack of comic books. We began to talk.

Like me he lived in Brooklyn. It was his fifth time at Burning Man. He had just gotten a haircut at a salon theme camp. Since we were in the library we talked about books. We talked about a book called *The World Without Us*, which describes what would happen if humanity suddenly disappeared: how nature would reclaim the planet, how our cities would decay, how long it would take the effects of global warming to fully mature, how long plastic would remain. We talked about megafauna, which are mentioned in *The World Without Us*, how the nice thing about megafauna was that they had coincided with human history—that even six thousand years ago there were still small woolly mammoths living on an island off Alaska. He wondered how dinosaurs had overtaken megafauna in the popular imagination. We talked about the Long Now Foundation in San Francisco, an organization started by Stewart Brand, founder of the *Whole*

Earth Catalog, who is trying to genetically resurrect megafauna.
I talked about how I had gone to see Charles C. Mann, the author
of the books *1491* and *1493,* speak at the Long Now Foundation.
He had listened to the podcast. We talked about *1493,* about how
in North America, before the Columbian exchange, there were
no earthworms, and how the Spanish had hired samurai to fight
the Aztecs in Mexico, and how somebody should make a movie
about that. We talked about Narnia and Ursula K. Le Guin. He
was reading *The Wizard of Earthsea.* We talked about how Le
Guin was an anarchist and a polyamorist. He told me that when
Le Guin was a child, her family had sheltered the last Native
American living a traditional life in California, who had wandered one day from the forest into the parking lot of a grocery
store. I asked if it was the same man described by Claude Levi-
Strauss in *Tristes Tropiques.* It was, he said.

I really belonged in the library! As helpful as the advice guru
had been, I decided I should only ever try to make friends in li-
braries from now on. The next time I came to Burning Man I
would make a beeline to the Black Rock City library, a direct
vector to the heart of things.

He was going to try and go to have a steam bath, he now said.
Did I want to come? If we got there before it opened at noon we
would have a good chance of avoiding the line. As we walked to
the steam bath theme camp, we introduced ourselves. Let's call
him Lunar Fox, which wasn't his name, but sounds like a name
someone would make up for Burning Man. I asked him how old
he was. He did not want to say. "I'm thirty-two," I volunteered.
"I'm thirty-three," he said.

We arrived at the steam bath just after noon. There was no
line. The man in charge gave us each a red wooden stake. "You're
the last two!" he said. We would have about an hour before he
would be calling people with red stakes to the steam bath. It

seemed serendipitous. "He probably says that to everyone," my new friend said.

We walked to his camp. It was called Desperado and was vaguely cowboy themed, or at least had a pair of saloon doors at its entryway. He prepared a funnel with coffee for me and went to do something. I waited for the water to boil. Twenty-somethings from Santa Cruz milled around, eating apples and putting hazelnut milk in their coffee. I watched one young man give another a pill capsule filled with white powder. "What is it?" asked the recipient. The other man shrugged. "Sparkle dust," said the guy, and swallowed the pill. I had not yet figured out how to get drugs at Burning Man. I had hoped they would simply appear. Instead a tall blond twenty-something man walked in and asked if anybody had any sunscreen. When my friend returned I was rubbing sunscreen on his broad, tan back. I prepared my coffee and we walked back to the steam bath.

We arrived just as our turn was called. We stripped naked and stood in line. The sun felt good on our naked bodies. We were given umbrellas to stand under. The steam bath was in a hexayurt. We stayed inside for a while. It was a collegial atmosphere, with people singing songs and spraying each other with a hose. We met a guy from Mongolia. We washed off the dust with Dr. Bronner's peppermint soap. Afterward, the ovenlike desert air felt cool. We dried in the sun, then put on our clothes again. We decided, next, to go to the orgy dome, something one could do only as part of a "couple or moresome." First we had to get my bike.

To get my bike I had to tell Adam something about where I was going. I introduced him to Lunar Fox. I figured Adam had his own conquests. His tan had deepened and he wore only a small pair of shiny golden shorts. *Feel the jealousy*, I told myself, looking at him.

On the way to the orgy dome we stopped at a *Miami Vice*–themed party for some drinks and snacks. The door was manned by a white guy and a black guy dressed as Crockett and Tubbs. I got a rum cocktail. Lunar Fox got water. Lunar Fox, it turned out, did not drink. We sat among pillows in an empty inflatable swimming pool and smiled at each other.

We had not discussed our purpose for going to the orgy dome. We had, after all, just met. The orgy dome was said to be air-conditioned, but it was barely air-conditioned. We were handed a bag with condoms, lube, wipes, mint Life Savers, and instructions for how to dispose of our materials afterward. We entered the dome. I was disappointed that there wasn't much of an orgy. In fact, it was all heterosexual couples having sex with each other. Lunar Fox and I sat on a couch and watched. We felt strange. It was clear that we should either do something or leave.

"Should we have sex?" I asked.

"Yes . . ." he said. "Do you want to?"

"Yes," I said.

"Are you sure?" he said.

"Yes," I said. The woman who greeted us at the door had advised us to express loud, enthusiastic consent.

When we left the dome, we walked over to a nearby shade structure where sitar music was playing. We sat in two camping chairs and talked about our experience. A woman who said she was from Columbus, Ohio, came by with a pitcher of iced coffee and offered us some. I accepted. It was cold and delicious, made with sweetened condensed milk. I offered some to Lunar Fox, who sniffed it and looked tempted but ultimately said no. He tried to be entirely straight edge, he said. The only time he allowed himself drugs was at Burning Man. He was an anarchist. He tried to live as closely to his political principles as possible, which meant, in part, not partaking of things that come from thousands of miles away, like coffee. He also forbid himself from watching porn, did not have a cell phone, and made a point of trying to get by on as little paid employment as possible, as a sort of protest.

I asked him why he did not watch porn. He said he thought it messed up his mind. We talked about the differences between male and female sexuality. I said I thought men and women wanted sex equally, but maybe the female body has a hard time having sex repeatedly. I was, at that moment, thinking of my own body, which felt tired.

"It's frustrating, because I could have sex three more times today, if my body could take it," I said.

"I could have sex five more times," he said.

He said the thing about sex was that if you don't have it for a long time your drive for it wanes, but if you have it once then you want to have it all the time again. Lunar Fox said that in all the times he had been to Burning Man he had never had sex or made out with anyone. I found this impossible. "It's easier to be a woman here," he said. I was not so sure. There were so many beautiful, naked bodies prancing around.

We both felt tired. He said that if he doesn't nap after sex, he spends the rest of the day trying to recapture the opportunity to nap. We talked about how sex wakes women up and makes men tired. It felt like a relief to throw out some generalities along gendered lines. Just throw them out there, lazily, without having to take the position I try to take when I am writing, that there are no such entities as "men" and "women," just spectrums of behavior and of being in the world, that can be shifted by technology and synthetic hormones.

We left the sitar tent, got on our bicycles, and cycled toward the playa. We wanted to look at a sculptural re-creation of Russia's *Mir* space station. We found it and went inside. One of the

Russians who built it was dismantling the lights. The space station was going to be set on fire later that night. We went and talked to him. He was dour, as one hopes a Russian to be. "First time in America. First time at Burning Man," he said with a thick accent. We asked if he would take Burning Man back to Russia. "There is no place like this in Russia," he said. "There would be rain."

We left the space station, bicycling toward the Temple of Whollyness, where some friends of friends of his were due to be married that afternoon. We passed a Mayan pyramid topped with the giant thumbs-up of a Facebook "like," which would later be set on fire. Lunar Fox told me about the first time he had come to Burning Man, in 1999. None of this had yet existed—Facebook likes, cell phone cameras, Russian delegations. Burning Man was smaller then, just serious environmental activist types with a hard-core leave-no-trace ethic. But it was the same, he said. Anybody who said it had changed was wrong. It was just bigger now, and as any society grows it experiences the same stratification, the same problems.

The temple was also a pyramid. Inside, objects from religious traditions had been removed from their history, thrown together in a panspiritual mixture of, well, whollyness. A Buddhist anvil dominated the center of the room, around which several hundred people sat on the floor in silent meditation. Gongs on the walls struck in automatic intervals. Outside, Burners had decorated the walls with shrines to people who had died, pets who had died, problems they were trying to let go of. I looked at photo collages of people with their dead mothers, brothers, and friends. All of this love, so poorly managed, so rarely expressed. I looked at Lunar Fox and we both had tears in our eyes.

We couldn't find the wedding we were looking for, but someone was getting married, and we cheered them. Afterward, sitting together in the sun and dust, we assembled a plywood hexagonal structure that joined with other hexagonal structures in a plywood molecule. We were supposed to write something on it, but we did not write anything. We watched it placed with the others and then we left. On Sunday it would be set on fire.

The day was fading. "This is normally when I go back to take a nap, but this day . . ." said Lunar Fox. "I don't know what to do about this day."

I knew what he meant. I had never had a day like this in my life. I had never become so close to someone so quickly. We visited a geodesic dome. We went to a chapel containing an organ that Lunar Fox wanted to play before it was set on fire that night. Inside, more people were getting married. He picked out "Here Comes the Bride" on the organ and we cheered the happy couple. Then we biked back to Desperado. We shared his dinner, a grilled cheese sandwich with some tomato soup. He said to stop by later, that maybe he would have some mushrooms. I stopped by later. He was wearing leather shorts, no shirt, and an aviator cap. He had no spare mushrooms. "The girl I made out with last night was just here," he said. I was confused . . . hadn't he said . . . ? It did not matter. I had my own complications. We made plans to meet at noon the next day. I didn't keep the rendezvous.

Instead I went back to my RV, where it turned out there had been drugs all the time. We put half a hit of a synthetic psychedelic under our lips and proceeded out into the night, the chemicals leaching from the paper as *Mir* was set on fire, the wedding chapel set on fire, the Facebook "like" set on fire. We wandered through the LED-infused landscape, its color palette that of the movie *Tron*, a vision of the future that had now become the future, a future filled with electronic dance music.

The drug hit us when we were playing beneath an art installation of rushing purple lights. We ran and danced in the lights, laughing and gasping. We boarded mutant vehicles, one shaped like a giant terrapin, one a postapocalyptic pirate ship called the *Thunder Gumbo*. We danced atop the vehicles. Beneath us the Burners on bicycles orbited like phosphorescent deep sea crustaceans. The memory of my day kept coming back to me. I kept thinking I was seeing people having sex, then realized I had just seen a pileup bike crash. I kept thinking I had met the people around me before. We put more paper under our lips.

We encountered a phone booth from which we could call God. I picked up the phone and spoke to God.

"Good morning," said God.

"Is it morning?" I asked.

"It's morning where you are," said God.

"Where are you?" I asked.

"I'm everywhere," said God.

"This is why people don't like you anymore!" I wailed, and hung up the phone.

I pictured God as an aged Burner somewhere near Palo Alto, who could not make it to Burning Man this year, who had instead rigged this magical telephone. I pictured volunteers like him across the country, awaiting phone calls so that they could play God and have contact with the magic of the playa. I considered that in fact probably the phone was rigged to someone in a tent nearby.

I began to see conspiracy. A mutant vehicle pulled up alongside us. On top I could see several older people, in their fifties and sixties. I saw them as aristocrats. They seemed to be wearing Aztec mohawks and Louis XVI–style powdered wigs. They were Brahmin priests observing us from on high, a whollyness of all elites in history. Their vehicle, shaped like a rainbow-colored anglerfish, was called the *Disco Fish*, and it was self-piloted by programmable GPS. Its scales were the primary colors of the Google logo. I saw the *Disco Fish* as a secret plot by Google to defy Burn-ing Man's anticorporate ethos with its self-driven cars, the project overseen by the executives on the second tier. My suspicions seemed confirmed when one of their number began discussing a show at the Guggenheim with one of my friends.

Still, we rode on the *Disco Fish*. We danced. We stayed up until the sun rose. We slowly made our way back to the RV, where we stayed and talked. Each of us had experienced a unity. One of our number had just left the company he had founded, fully vested. He no longer had to work, ever. He told us about all the things he had thought about this year, when a job that once seemed magical was transformed into a grind, with an office, with rules, where he realized he no longer belonged and was no longer wanted until, the day before he left for Burning Man, he was paid to leave. He wore a hat that said "Junior Airline Pilot." While we sat there, outside the RV, Adam returned. He wore blue leggings and a white fur vest. Someone had painted his face. He was exuberant. He had biked to the edge of the playa and watched the sun rise. I hugged him. I was so happy to see him. Another person had gone to a sunrise party on the outer playa called Robot Heart, where Shervin Pishevar, the venture capitalist who had once shaved the logo of the startup Uber on the side of his head, was dancing on top of the sound system. The corporate lawyer arrived, wearing Superman boxers and a bikini.

No wonder people hate Burning Man, I thought, when I pic-tured it as a cynic might: rich people on vacation breaking rules that everyone else would suffer for if they didn't obey. The hypocrisy of the "creative autonomous zone" weighed on me. Many of these people would go back to their lives and back to work on the great farces of our age. They wouldn't argue for the decriminalization of the drugs they had used; they wouldn't want anyone to know about their time in the orgy dome. That they had cheered at the funeral pyre of a Facebook "like" wouldn't play well on Tuesday in the cafeteria at Facebook. The people who accumulated the surplus value of the world's photographs, "life events," and ex-boyfriend obsessions were now celebrating their freedom from the web they'd entangled all of us in, the freedom to exist without the Internet. Plus all this crap—the polyester fur leg warmers and plastic water bottles and disposable batteries—this garbage made from harvested hydrocarbons that will never disappear.

To protest these things in everyday life bore a huge social cost—one that only people like Lunar Fox were willing to grimly undertake—and maybe that's what the old Burners disliked about the new ones: the new ones upheld the idea of autonomous zones. The $400 ticket price was as much about the right to leave what happened at Burning Man behind as it was to enter in the first place.

Still, this place felt right. I had been able to do things here that I had wanted to do for a long time, that I never could have done at home. And if this place felt right, if it had expanded so much over the years because to so many people it felt like "home," it had something to do with the inadequacy of the old social structures that still governed our lives in our real homes, where we felt lonely, isolated, and unable to form the connections we wanted.

If I had to predict a future, it would be that Burning Man would last only as long as we did, the last generation that lived some part of life without the Internet, who were trying to adjust our reality to our technology. Younger people, I hoped, would not need autonomous zones. Their lives would be free of timidity. They would do their new drugs and have their new sex. They wouldn't think of themselves as women or men. They would meld their bodies seamlessly with their machines, without our embarrassment, without our notions of authenticity.

I had been awake for more than twenty-four hours. I would not be able to sleep for many hours more. I was ready for the feelings to stop now, but they just kept going.

BIRTH CONTROL AND REPRODUCTION

The inadequacy of birth control technology does not need to be explained. Women's lives are linked to pills and devices that cause weight gain, spontaneous bleeding, lowering of sexual desire, bad skin, blood clots, varicose veins, and depression. A woman might invest in an expensive or invasive technology, only to discover that it does not serve her and must be removed for something else. We use birth control because it can prevent pregnancy, endometriosis, ovarian cancer, acne. Still, one goes to the doctor to learn about one's "options" with a sense of dismal resignation to their various imperfections. Almost half of American women will have an unintended pregnancy before the age of forty-five; three in ten will have an abortion.

I went on the pill at eighteen, when I first started having sex. For the next ten years I cycled through pills and more pills. Some made my skin bad. Some made me gain weight. Some were covered by health insurance and then suddenly not. Some diminished my interest in sex entirely. I suspected they exacerbated the depression I experienced in my twenties, which I treated instead with other kinds of pills. At the age of twenty-eight, after a decade on the pill, a doctor informed me that I should not have been taking pills with estrogen at all, since I occasionally have migraines with aura, which puts me at increased risk for a stroke in the event of a blood clot. I went off the pills and did not get my period again for six months.

When I next had a boyfriend and got tired of condoms, I installed a hormone-free copper intrauterine device, which eventually made my periods last twice as long. A doctor suggested menopausal hormones to deal with the bleeding and that did nothing. I took a progesterone mini-pill that made me bleed for two months straight, a relatively common side effect of the mini-pill that made sex embarrassing and clearly repelled my partners. It seemed impossible that in this era of advanced technology I was still reliant on the whims of a contraption that was literally elementary, a copper device that had been invented forty years ago.

When I went to have the IUD removed things got worse. The nylon filaments by which an IUD is pulled out had been cut too short; there was no sign of the thing. First I paid for a sonogram to see if it was still in my uterus (it was), then I visited a series of doctors who fretted unhelpfully or contemplated surgery until finally one successfully managed to remove it. All the birth control options left to me had potential for side effects and cost upward of $500. While most devices were covered under the regulations of the Affordable Care Act, the testing to make sure I did not have an infection before the IUD was inserted was not. There were always condoms. "And how realistic is it that you will consistently use condoms?" asked one doctor. I had a boyfriend by then, so for a while relied on his self-control, but I really did not want to have a baby. I got a plastic IUD with hormones in it, a technology that had been invented in the 1970s. For six months, I bled off and on until suddenly, miraculously, my body settled into something approaching stability.

We tend to think of technology as something that we invent and direct to our own ends, and machines as prosthetics that we deploy, but sometimes we conform our expectations to the technology that we inherit. This is especially true of contraception, which has seen almost no paradigm-changing innovation in the past forty years. We take as a given the limitation that the condom is the only contraceptive that protects against both pregnancy and sexually transmitted infection. We take as a given that the best ways to prevent a pregnancy are the worst ways to prevent infections. We accept the lack of options for women who cannot take hormones. We treat as exceptional the risks for people who want to get pregnant but whose partners have chronic viruses. The last advancement in contraceptive technology for men came after the invention of latex in 1920.

In 1995, the Institute of Medicine issued a report calling for "a second contraceptive revolution." It cited the above shortcomings, and public health issues such as the high rate of unintended pregnancies and abortions in the United States and around the world, rapid population growth, and the difficulties poorer and medically underserved communities have in accessing satisfactory contraception. The twenty years since then have been punctuated by breakthroughs in everything from computing to theoretical physics to decoding the human genome. None of the above problems have been solved.

Private-sector investment into birth control has dramatically fallen from its peak in the 1970s. The biggest pharmaceutical and biotechnology companies have largely abandoned research in the field. It is not in a pharmaceutical company's best interest to innovate away from a profitable and widely used once-a-day pill and toward a long-acting, cheaper alternative. Because contraceptives are taken by wide populations of healthy people, the barriers for testing and regulatory approval are high. What innovation there has been in recent decades has largely come from the government, or from philanthropic organizations such as the Gates Foundation.

Changes in sexual behavior—more partners on average, longer periods of sexual activity outside of marriage—coincided with the decrease in funding for research into contraception. The technologies we use today were invented for a different era of sexual morals. I rarely considered, when undergoing another lecture by a physician about "risky" sexual behavior (namely sex without a condom), that I was experiencing the consequences of a research paradigm rooted in the expectations of half a century ago. For decades, prevention of sexually transmitted infections was considered an endeavor separate from that of pregnancy prevention, the assumption being that infections were not a concern for the "normative majority"—the committed couples concerned with moderating fertility but at lower risk for STIs. In reading old research papers about contraception, emphasis is consistently placed on modifying behavior to conform to the limitations of the technology, rather than modifying technology in consideration of a wider range of sexual behavior.

Fighting for the right to merely get birth control had taken so much energy we had apparently forgotten to make any other demands. We had set our sights very low, especially considering that contraception was one of those advancements of civilization, like literacy or dental hygiene, that would not be taken back.

Birth control is the original fusion between the human body and our technology, the initiation of a symbiosis that will only accelerate in the future. For the overwhelming majority of Americans, population control is the default setting, the one that we will maintain for most of our adult lives, diverting from it only for an average of 1.7 pregnancies in the United States. And yet it's the brief windows when women pursue the maximum fertility of their bodies that are often treated as their "natural" state. Perhaps what hinders our thinking on the subject the most is this commitment to an obsolete idea of biological destiny, initiated with the false menstrual periods of the early birth control pill, enshrined forever in 28-day plastic packages that force women to return to the pharmacy according to the waxing and waning of the lunar month. And, despite advances toward mandated coverage, this universal question remains a disproportionate financial burden, considered a personal cost borne by one half of the population rather than the other. Framing birth control as a choice, and not as a human right, had caused us to settle not only for mediocre technology and poor availability, but it had encouraged us to think of our childless lives as an arrested state.

Today, one in five American adults is childless, compared with one in ten in the 1970s. Between 2007 and 2011, the fertility rate in the United States declined by 9 percent. The average number of babies per woman reached a record low in 2013. Babies are increasingly thought of as choices. I am approaching the age now where if I don't have a baby I will have chosen not to have a baby. I think: *Did I make a choice?*

One sweltering August night in Manhattan in 2015, I accompanied a friend into her bedroom, leaving my boyfriend and her male roommate in the living room, where they were watching an arm-wrestling tournament on ESPN. I read out the instructions while she prepared an injection, then I sat back on her neatly made bed and watched her across the room. She had her back to a mirror, jeans shorts pulled down. She frowned as she looked over her shoulder to find the right angle. The injection had to be intramuscular. She had learned at a three-hour workshop how to check for air bubbles, how not to hit a vein. She had drawn a dot with a marker on the right spot, where the rivet on the back pocket of her jeans would normally be. She gave herself the shot. Then she sat down on the bed. She was very pale.

Her fertility doctors called this massive dose of hormones the "trigger shot." After days of preparation this shot catalyzed her ovaries to release several eggs at once. The injection would be successful if a pregnancy test the next day showed up positive, a pseudo-pregnancy that indicated the flood of synthetic hormones now coursing through her veins. Thirty-six hours after her shot, I accompanied my friend to a clinic in Manhattan, where her eggs were "harvested" and cryogenically frozen. The nurse had warned her about the "sad faces" in the waiting room, of people whose fertility treatments were unsuccessful. The people trying to prolong their fertility and those attempting to revive it went to the same doctors.

All of this was so new. The FDA had removed the "experimental" label from egg freezing only in 2012. In 2013, 5,000 women froze their eggs. By 2018, that number was expected to be as many as 76,000 per year. Also in 2014, Facebook and Google announced they would cover the cost for employees to freeze their eggs. My wealthier friends started doing it in 2015, paying out of pocket. A cycle of egg freezing cost as much as $10,000, plus a $500 annual fee for the cryogenic storage. Sometimes it took more than one round to successfully produce and collect the eggs. Then, if the woman later opted to try to get pregnant with her frozen eggs, she would have to spend many thousands of dollars more for in vitro fertilization. As with all in vitro fertilization, the majority of attempts to get pregnant do not result in live births.

It was as if we had made something very simple incredibly complicated. Here were these bodies, ready to reproduce, controlled against reproduction, then stimulated for an eventual reproduction that was put on ice. My friends who wanted to prolong their fertility did so, now that they were in their thirties and professionally successful, because circumstances in their lives had not lined up as planned. They had excelled at their jobs. They had nice apartments and enough money to comfortably start a family, but they lacked a domestic companion who would provide the necessary genetic material, lifelong support, and love. They wanted to be the parents they had grown up under, but love couldn't be engineered, and ovaries could.

Hanging over all of this was an idea of choice, an arbitrary linking of goals and outcomes, which reduced structural economic, technological, and social change to an individual decision. "The right to choose"—the right to birth control and abortion services—is different from the idea of choice I mean here. I mean that the baby question justified a fiction that one had to conform one's life to a uniform box by a certain deadline. If the choice were only to have a baby or not, then anybody who wanted a baby and was physically able would simply have one (as many people did), but what I saw with my friends was that it wasn't actually about the choice of having a baby but of setting up a nuclear family, which unfortunately could not, unlike making a baby, happen more or less by fiat.

I would have daydreams about a doctor shaking her head and

telling me that there was no way I could ever have children, at which point I would be sad but at least freed from marriage. I could just live my life according to its drift without ever having to make a "decision" to conform back into the type of family in which I had been raised for the purpose of setting up a stable environment for a child. The question of meeting a "life partner" mattered less when I gave up on the idea of children, because I saw no particular reason or need to set up a household with someone if I didn't have a child. But then I would think about the next forty years, a long road, and that I had already enjoyed plenty of adventures and accomplished most of what I had wanted to do, and spending part of that time caring for a child appealed to me. There was never a moment where I felt like if I "chose" to have a baby, what I considered the necessary precondition for having a baby—someone who wanted to have a baby with me—would have automatically appeared. Of course I could have chosen, and could still choose, to raise a child on my own. Many women do this, and to pretend they don't pay a great penalty for doing so is to succumb to sentimentalism. I didn't have to get married to have a baby, but our society was set up economically and socially in ways that make it difficult to raise a child as a single person. The cost of giving birth in the United States is expensive, on average three times the cost of that in other countries. The infant mortality rate is the highest of the twenty-seven wealthiest countries in the world, and higher for black women. The United States is one of only three countries in the world that does not guarantee paid parental leave.

Are we choosing? My friends who have frozen their eggs do not feel like they have chosen—they want to have babies. My friends who want to get pregnant but whose bodies will not cooperate do not feel like they have chosen. When we were young and in our twenties and on birth control were we really making a choice not to start a family? It never felt like that. It felt more like a family had not chosen us.

After women have babies, they begin to lose equality. According to the Bureau of Labor Statistics, childless, unmarried women make 96 cents for every dollar a man makes. As women bear children, one study found that they would suffer a "wage penalty" in relation to men of 4 percent per child, a penalty that increases on the lower end of the income spectrum. When it comes to having children, some women see this moment of resignation as noble and beautiful; many women do not. Or they simply tell themselves that they will be eager to take on such a role at some point, only to find, when their late thirties come along, that what they will sacrifice looms as great or even greater than it ever did.

The news is full of information about a crisis of fertility, of many women "waiting until the last minute" to have babies, although what's certain is that with every technological advancement that allows an increase in female childbearing age the longer women will want to wait. Think of the calculation: on the one hand you have the life that you have known, and the sexual experience you have accrued. On the other you have the assertion of a love that outperforms all other forms of love, and of an instinctual response that will allow for an easy conformation to the reduction in professional status a woman will experience by becoming a parent. As with marriage, the promise of emotional fulfillment is based on an almost religious faith in a future different from one's experience to date. Also like marriage, raising a child is a process that's purported to have escaped history, such that all interest in sexual freedom will suddenly cease for the purpose of having a baby.

Futurism, when it comes to reproduction, is not only about cryogenics. The infinite prolongation of fertility is a false future; a future that truly reconciles family and sexual freedom would be one more supportive of single parents, not just materially but ideologically. As a line of inquiry, this futurism would recognize that marriage and babies have no necessary link. It would consider how to ungender reproduction and child care but ensure that children have masculine and feminine influences in their lives; how to make workplaces and schedules more amenable to caretaking; how to legally establish co-parenting commitments outside the framework of marriage. This experiment is already under way: 40 percent of births in the United States are to unwed parents. This happened because most people have separated their sex lives from marriage, but the thinking about the subject has yet to flip. When people cite the research about the advantages of raising a child in a two-parent home, it tends to be an argument for marriage, not for improving the experience of raising a child outside of it. And this has meant that many women, unmarried but also pragmatic about the challenges of single parenthood, feel the "choice" they have made not to have a child is not much of a choice at all.

From a personal standpoint, the sacrifices it would take for me to have a child by myself, using genetic material from a friend or a sperm donor, outweigh my desire to have a child. I can, however, picture an arrangement with a man I love and care about but don't want to marry, someone who also wants to have a child, organizing from birth the custodial arrangements that divorced and never-married people have been honing for decades to raise children. For the first year, perhaps, we would commit to living in the same house together, but then agree that the shared project of raising a child does not have to come with a committed love for each other.

Or I just won't have a baby at all. To be religious is often associated with a certain idea of family, but most religions have allowed for the declaration of a vocation based on one's sexual practices. Married life was one such vocation, one way of being in the world. There were also the figures of the hermit, the monk, the ascetic, the nun. Celibacy was traditionally required to follow these roles, which were defined by either severe introspection and isolation or an equally radical commitment of one's life to the public, to serving the community. Their roles outside family were respected by society, because of collective acknowledgment that presenting to the world as an individual allowed for orders of connection unavailable to people busy raising and providing for their offspring. Now there is a new kind of person, perhaps in a similar position, whose place apart from the householder is assured not by celibacy but by contraception. Is this not also a vocation?

FUTURE SEX

Five years passed, and my life saw few structural changes. I was, however, changed. I now understood the fabrication of my sexuality. I saw the seams of its construction and the arbitrary nature of its myths. I came to understand that sexuality had very little to do with the sex you actually had. A straight woman who hooked up with people she met online in her search for a boyfriend was not different, in behavior, from the gay man who made a public declaration about looking for noncommittal sex. The man who cheated on his wife was no different, in action, from the polyamorist who slept with someone outside of his primary relationship. It was the ideation and expression of intent that differentiated sexualities, not the actual sex. A futuristic sex was not going to be a new kind of historically unrecognizable sex, just a different way of talking about it.

I came to have a heightened perception of the power the traditional story had over the sense of my standing in the world, especially when I traveled to places where the old social order was intact, where small talk began with "Are you married?" or "Do you have children?" I wondered if I would be happier if I could answer yes. I liked my life, but I knew I would also like the ease with which having a family could be explained, the universal approval with which it was met.

To declare that I would organize my sexuality around the principle of free love seemed at times like a pointless statement. I was unsure a declaration of pursuit had any effect on lived experience. Just as wanting to fall in love did not manifest love, proclaiming myself "sexually free" would not liberate me from inhibition. A life lived with the goal of having a wide range of non-exclusive erotic friendships would still have long stretches of monogamy. I would still have to respect the preferences of my sexual partners. I could not override feelings with a claim to freedom. I knew, however, that naming sexual freedom as an ideal put the story I told myself about my life in greater alignment with the choices I had already made. It offered continuity between my past and the future. It gave value to experiences that I had viewed with frustration or regret. Without such a declaration of purpose we were living a double standard. We could talk about coregasms, but we believed in the nobility of abstinence. We wanted gender equality, but we wanted the man to pick up the check. We wanted babies, but we thought we needed to get married to have them. These contradictions resulted in a greater duplicity, where what was good or bad in sex was not about the sex at all, but rather where the sex would land us in the social order. I had disliked my freedom because I didn't want to see myself landing on the outside of normal.

I had always preferred success through recognized channels: getting good grades, going to the right college. I experienced satisfaction in obeying rules, and I had greater affirmation from my family when we acted as if I hadn't chosen to be alone, when we spoke as if I was simply waiting (maybe for decades) for the right person to come along. It was easier to see my circumstances as the result of unluckiness, rather than deliberate sabotage from a willful declaration not to pursue lifelong partnership. And then there was always the possibility that I was just an undesirable woman trying to cast a more flattering light on my circumstances, or that I was naive and would learn another lesson about the pursuit of sexual freedom being emotionally destructive. I began to ignore these arguments, or at least I had now absorbed a powerful lesson about resistance to change: that it manifests less by institutional imposition and more by the subtle suggestions of the people who love you.

Some people would remain committed to the institution of marriage, but I hoped that married partnership would cease to be seen as a totalizing end point and instead become something more modest, perhaps an institutional basis for shared endeavors such as raising children or making art. Open marriages had already lost stigma. Practice would make us better at the emotional management of multiple concurrent relationships. We would have more overt experience in free love, more evidence to work with. "Failed" marriages would no longer be interpreted as personal failure.

I found that I wanted all that, but mostly I wanted to live in a world with a wider range of sexual identities. I hoped the primacy and legitimacy of a single sexual model would continue to erode as it has, with increasing acceleration, in the past fifty years.

I spent only a few months in San Francisco, but the city just happened to be a synecdoche, where the post-1960s combination of computers and sexual diversity was especially concentrated. It was like Epcot, in a way, an experimental prototype city of tomorrow informed by queerness and dedicated to sexual experimentation. You could tour it and leave with a showcase world of sexual options in mind.

I first went to San Francisco in 2012. Then I left. When I returned a couple years later, San Francisco felt different. Nobody wore Google T-shirts anymore. Protesters had begun throwing rocks at the buses that took employees down to the peninsula. The city was going through some changes, shedding a carapace that had kept it in the past. Peace signs still hung in the windows of the head shops and thrift stores on Haight Street, but the city kept getting sleeker, more expensive, more uniform in appearance.

On this visit I stayed at the apartment in the Mission of a computer programmer whom I had met on OkCupid back in 2012. Now we were friends, and he offered the use of his place while he went east to train for a new job. Before he left, we spent an afternoon walking around the city. We walked to Dolores Park, dazed in the sunshine of the longest drought in California history. My friend ordered a tofu banh mi from a food truck. We sat in the grass in the warm January sun next to a woman wearing socks, sandals, and a mélange of colorful scarves. We watched as she encountered a man similarly attired, and the way that they saluted each other made us exchange glances.

"Now we're going to hear people talk about some things that aren't real," my companion said. He was the sort of person who had actually tried to find medical evidence for the medicinal properties of kombucha (very little, it turned out). He had disdain for the apparent suspension of reason he saw practiced around him.

We took a bus to Golden Gate Park, then walked to Hippie Hill and smoked a joint. In front of us, a pod of crust punks dozed peacefully on a picnic blanket, holding the leash of a velvety tabby cat that stared up at the trees in a state of perpetual alarm. One of the punks, her dreadlocks covered in a scarf, stood up and began hula hooping in a desultory manner. If you took away the signifiers of a crust punk (velvety dogs and cats, hula hoops) would they just be ordinary homeless people? Does political intention make a crust punk different from a mentally ill person, or a drug addict? It was the same old question, whether a declaration of purpose might protect you from failure. The sun setting in our eyes and the drone of a nearby drum circle produced in me a low-level nausea. A man on Rollerblades tried to sell us one of his glass pipes. My friend wondered if most of the people on Rollerblades in the park were selling things. We stood up and went to Amoeba Records.

On the bus home, a man with leathery tan skin and long hair yelled at everyone around him about the villainy of our cell phones. "Do you know where the metal in that thing came from?" he said, glaring at a young woman with a phone in her hand. "Have you heard of fire and brimstone?" He pronounced us morons; yelled that the phones were starting wars; described hellish mines and rare-earth minerals. He tried hitting on the woman he had antagonized, asking her out on a date. "I'm from New Zealand," he concluded angrily, and got off the bus. He had not spoken with a discernable accent. "Like nobody's ever heard of New Zealand," my friend said.

My host left and I dutifully watered his bamboo twice a week, his succulents once a week, and carefully rinsed the epiphytes under the faucet. I did all my favorite California things. I drank expensive cappuccinos, ate cheap tacos, and listened to his carefully organized collection of house music. Most of the records featured tuneless singing in German or French over synthesized beats. I thought about the little jar he had shown me in a drawer, containing several Altoid mints covered in tinfoil, which he said I should feel free to try, if I felt like it.

One day, on a Thursday around midday, I took one. I lay on the bed and watched patterns emerge on the white wall in front of me. I felt the sun passing through the windows, filtering between the leafy plants and pressing on my eyelids. I ate a cookie and wrote a line in a notebook about "a post-cookie lull, a feeling I had acknowledged but never admitted to." I took more useful notes: "Feeling of being led to a sandbox by a child, dumped, and playing with incredibly heavy sand," and: "Mind still empty, revolving like a bicycle in an empty velodrome around all the old concerns."

Several hours in, I walked toward Dolores Park to sit on the grassy hill. I walked down Eighteenth Street alongside the strollers, passing the tourists eating pastries outside Tartine and pizza at Delfina. I sat in the grass in the park. I was looking at my phone to look normal when a squadron of women flew around me from behind. They ran down the hill in formation, dressed in matching tank tops and short shorts, dispensing Red Bull to picnickers from canisters worn on their backs like rocket boosters. I went back to the apartment and longed for a tactile dome with a light show to amuse me. I did not feel very introspective, only bored and restless. Ten hours in, when I thought I could act sufficiently normal, I went to Bi-Rite and bought an ice cream.

On my last Friday in town, I used Google to map a route to Menlo Park and went to lunch with a friend who worked at Facebook. Via public transportation, it took something like two hours to get to Facebook, riding first the BART and then switching to the top deck of a clanging red double-decker CalTrain that vented hot air as it rolled prehistorically along El Camino Real. On a city bus from the train station toward Facebook HQ, the bus stopped at a Veterans' Hospital—the same Menlo Park Veterans' Hospital, I presumed, where Ken Kesey had taken LSD for the first time. It seemed impossible that anything of cultural import had fermented in such a wasteland but it was here, and within a few miles of here, that it had all happened: the People's Computer Company, the creative writing grad students taking acid on Perry Lane, the offices of the *Whole Earth Catalog*, all of it as impossible to transplant to the Menlo Park of now as it was to overlay the memory of a down-and-out folk scene over the Chipotles and Juice Generations in Greenwich Village. After disembarking from the bus, I walked past a strip mall with a Jack-in-the-Box restaurant and a Starbuck's. Then the sidewalk dissolved into some sand along the shoulder of a busy six-lane road next to a construction site. The road reached its terminus at a giant thumbs-up, which marked the entrance to Facebook's offices. Before it was the kind of hellish sun-beaten multifaceted pedestrian intersection that exists only in suburban environments where there are no pedestrians. I was late, and anxiously pressed buttons on poles to hasten the walk lights to the thumbs-up on the other side. I should have rented a car. They had apps for these situations.

I passed through Facebook's gates along a street called Hacker Way, the noise of the concrete outside muted into soft black asphalt. At midday, the parking lot that formed a perimeter around Facebook was filled with stationary cars and empty of people. Electric car chargers emitted a low hum. Perimeters within perimeters, one demanding a finger signature on a nondisclosure agreement drawn up on a glowing tablet computer, some Hi-Chews pilfered from the candy bowl next to it, past a flat-screen television on which a shiny-faced Mark Zuckerberg stood and lectured with the volume on mute, and then I was with my friend in the inner sanctum, the amusement park village with its simulacra of urbanity. In the screen-printing shop, an archive of Facebook propaganda hung on the wall, brightly colored hand-printed posters that read EVENTUALLY EVERYTHING CONNECTS, PRIDE CONNECTS US, SYSTEMS FOR SOCIETY, IF IT WORKS IT'S OBSOLETE, and, in traffic-light colors, SLOW DOWN AND FIX YOUR SHIT.

When Stewart Brand described Stanford's Artificial Intelligence lab in the pages of *Rolling Stone* in 1972, he described the beanbag room, the beards and long hair, the posters against the Vietnam War and Richard Nixon, and signs written in *Lord of the Rings* Elvish Feanorian script. He described hackers as "those magnificent men with their flying machines, scouting a leading edge of technology which has an odd softness to it; outlaw country, where rules are not decree or routine so much as the starker demands of what's possible." This was the feeling that Facebook was trying hard to convince itself it was keeping alive.

I left after a lunch of stuffed squash, quinoa, a green juice, and a papaya agua fresca, ejected back into the beating sun and traffic but this time holding a rolled-up poster of a wrench overlaid with the words "Nothing at Facebook Is Somebody Else's Problem" and with a button pinned to my tote bag that asked, "Is Connectivity a Human Right?" I waited under the fat droughty sun for a bus, then crossed into the shade of the Jack-in-the-Box and called a cab.

The beauty of science fiction was that its authors never had to work out the logistics of how we would arrive in the future. The future was presented as a fait accompli, and the difficult work by which a society accepted new social configurations did not have to be explained. From the vantage point of the present, it was easier to think that the future would be like *The Jetsons*, where families would look exactly the same, but labor would be outsourced to robots and intelligent appliances. The last fifty years of social movements had already rendered that vision of the future obsolete. At the very least, the Jetsons would be a two-income household.

I had spent most of my adult life looking for some scene that did not feel as if its stated ideals were thinly veiled sales pitches but I had found it only a handful of times, in the always-impermanent dynamics of particular groups of friends at particular moments in time, on psychedelics, in the wilderness, occasionally in writing. I had wanted to seek out a higher principle of life than the search for mere contentment, to pursue emotional experiences that could not be immediately transposed to a party of young people in a cell phone ad, even if it meant delving into ugliness, contracting an STD, or lifting my shirt to entice someone jerking off over the Internet. There was no industry of dresses and gift registries for the sexuality that interested me in these years, and some part of the reason I wanted to document what free love might look like was to reveal shared experiences of the lives we were living that fell outside a happiness that could be bought or sold.

America had a lot of respect for the future of objects, and less interest in the future of human arrangements. The history of the sexual vanguard in America was a long list of people who had been ridiculed, imprisoned, or subjected to violence. So it was annoying to hear the hubris of technologists, while knowing that gadgetry or convenience in telecommunication was the easy kind of futurism, the kind that attracted money. A real disruption or hack was a narration that did not make any sense to us the first time it was told, that would provoke too much repugnance to show in a cell phone ad.

To experience sexuality was to have a body that pursued a feeling, a dot in the distance toward which it must move. We wanted to follow the body into a more progressive future, to think there might be some intuition to rely upon, but the number of people any one life contained was finite. A data set was just a data set; the flying machines were carcasses of coltan and steel. The future was a discomfiting cultural story, and difficult to discern.

ACKNOWLEDGMENTS

For their help with this book, the author would like to thank Mitzi Angel, Edward Orloff, Lorin Stein, Keith Gessen, Christian Lorentzen, Mark Lotto, Yaddo, the MacDowell Colony, the Millay Center for the Arts, Lawrence Wilson and Rebekah Werth, Anna Lai, Tobias Bürger, Torsten Bender, Les and Ellen Hersh, Tao Lin, Jessica Wurst, Emily Brochin, the Power Broker Book Club, Chris Mancuso, and Stephen, Leonard, and Diana Witt.